Mother Nature's
CANDY
COOKBOOK

METRO BOOKS
New York

An Imprint of Sterling Publishing
387 Park Avenue South
New York, NY 10016

AUTHOR: Alison Candlin
EDITORS: Hazel Eriksson and Sam Kennedy
ASSISTANT EDITOR: Jo Morley
COOKERY CONSULTANT: Anne Sheasby
FOOD STYLIST: Donna Gregory
DESIGNER: Louise Turpin
PRODUCTION MANAGER: Rohana Yusof
PUBLISHER: Sarah Bloxham

ISBN 978-1-4351-5003-4

For information about custom editions, special sales, and premium and corporate purchases, please contact Sterling Special Sales at 800-805-5489 or specialsales@sterlingpublishing.com.

Printed in China

2 4 6 8 10 9 7 5 3 1

www.sterlingpublishing.com

Mother Nature's
CANDY
COOKBOOK

Alison Candlin

METRO BOOKS

CONTENTS

MAKING YOUR OWN NATURAL AND DELICIOUS CANDIES

Sweets are bad for you—everyone knows that. Or are they? All the candy recipes in this book contain fruits, herbs, spices, or even flowers that are fresh and give a hit of health-boosting nutrients and other active healing ingredients. And when you make candies yourself at home, you are in control of all the ingredients that have gone into them and can be certain that they are of the best possible quality. There are no artificial sweeteners, harmful additives, or synthetic colorings in the recipes within this book, so you can feel reassured that the treats you make for yourself, your children, or as gifts for family and friends are all natural, as well as delicious.

You'll also find that making your own is cheaper than buying mass-produced, commercial candies, as well as being better for you, rewarding and fun, and surprisingly easy. There are simple recipes here for all your sweet-shop favorites: smooth peppermint creams, luxurious truffles, fruity jellies, creamy fudge, and more.

Start with some simple basics before trying the more complicated sweets: perfect the technique of boiling a syrup to make Barley Sugar Twists (page 109) before you try pulled candies, like Pulled Mint Candies (page 100); or practice your basic fondant making with Chocolate Peppermint Creams (page 101) before attempting stuffed fondants, like Strawberry and Raspberry Creams (page 88).

CHOOSING YOUR INGREDIENTS

As with all cooking, your finished result can only be as good as the ingredients you have used. Don't skimp and buy the cheapest of everything or your efforts will be all but wasted. Sugar is the basic constituent of most candies, but there are so many different forms and types that there is no need for the flavor of your sweets to ever become boring. Black treacle or molasses give a dark sweetness with a back note of sharpness; fruit sugars have a fresh tang; brown sugar gives warmth, and superfine sugar, clarity. Always try to buy unrefined sugar, as this has a better flavor than processed white sugars, as well as a lovely natural color.

With chocolate, in particular, it is usually worth spending a little extra on good quality confectioner's chocolate (see page 31). Poor

SUGARED APPLE JELLY, PAGE 79

quality chocolate will not melt smoothly with a glossy finish and will not taste as good, either.

When choosing fruits, look for ones that are just ripe and in perfect condition—save any blemished fruits for making jellies or purées, where the condition of the flesh is less important. If you are using the skin, peel, or rind, choose fruits that have been grown organically and citrus fruits that are unwaxed. Always take great care if you are picking your own ingredients from the garden or hedgerow to be quite sure that what you choose is edible. If you are in any doubt about the identification of something, leave it well alone.

HEALING CANDIES

*F*or many minor ailments, such as a sore throat, tickly cough, or blocked nose, just the action of sucking on a sweet can help to make you feel better, by stimulating saliva production to lubricate the throat. Many over-the-counter remedies are actually little more than just a boiled sweet, and if you make your own you will reduce your reliance on commercial remedies and have something more delicious to suck on, too. Include some actively good ingredients, such as honey, lemon, or mint and you can help to soothe the problem fast and effectively.

A poorly child with a sore throat is sure to feel better with a Summer Fruit Lollipop (page 90) to lick or a Mint Lollipop (page 104) to suck. For grown-ups, Homemade Lemon Sweets (page 46 and opposite) or Pear Drops (page 78) will offer a fruity boost of vitamin C at the same time, or the menthol vapors from a batch of Herbal Healers (page 110) or Pulled Mint Candies (page 100) can help to clear congestion in the nose, sinus, or chest at the same time.

Mint is a tried-and-tested remedy for indigestion and the trick of sucking an after-dinner mint when you have over indulged is popular because it works. Pages 98–105 contain several recipes that can help, including Clear Mints (page 104) and Pulled Mint Candies (page 100).

Many of the ingredients within this book have even more powerful healing properties, and while this is most effective when you eat the fruits in their natural state, you can incorporate some of their goodness when you use them in your candies.Blueberries, for instance, are a superfood that can help to prevent urinary tract infections and may even help to promote brain health and slow down age-related memory loss—try including a few of your intake in the White Chocolate and Blueberry Fudge (page 94).

The pectin found in apples can help to reduce cholesterol and the risk of heart disease, and their boost of potassium can help to control blood pressure. You can make a batch of apples last by turning them into Apple

Leather (page 84) or a vibrant Green Apple Paste (page 85).

Even chocolate contains flavonoids with antioxidant properties that can help to keep your heart, veins, and arteries healthy by reducing your blood pressure and stress levels—just as long as you don't eat too much.

Each new ingredient section is introduced by a summary of the health benefits of the fruits, herbs or flowers that follow, and throughout the

book, 'Actively Good' boxes highlight specific healing properties of an ingredient used in a particular recipe.

Not only will the results of your homemade natural candies be deliciously indulgent, you can relax knowing that a little of what you fancy really can do you some good.

HOMEMADE LEMON SWEETS, PAGE 46

EQUIPMENT & TECHNIQUES

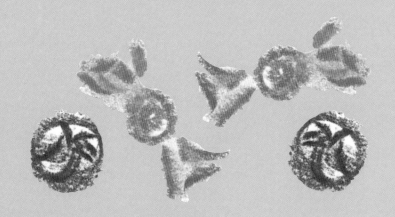

Basic Equipment

You don't need much equipment for making candies at home. For some, a bowl or work surface will suffice, and most can be made using equipment that you probably already have. Even specialized tools can be found in a good hardware or kitchen-ware store.

SAUCEPANS
Good quality, heavy, deep saucepans are the most important tool for successful candy making. Those made from cast-iron, copper, aluminum, or stainless steel are most suitable for the high temperatures reached when making sugar syrups. In a thin saucepan the syrup will heat unevenly and burn easily.

As the syrup will rise in the pan as it boils, be sure to choose a saucepan that has a capacity about four times as great as the amount of ingredients being used. Choose a deep one rather than a wide, shallow one.

The best way to clean a saucepan after it has been used for candy making is to fill it immediately with hot water and leave it to simmer, covered, until the syrup has dissolved.

CANDY THERMOMETER
A special thermometer that will withstand the temperature of a boiling, concentrated syrup makes successful candy making much easier. The graduations should be easy to read and calibrated from 60°F (16°C) to 360°F (182°C). Many have markings to indicate the various stages of the sugar-boiling process (see pages 20–21) and it is a good idea to choose one that clips to the side of the saucepan.

To 'season' a new thermometer, place it in a saucepan of cold water. Heat the water gently to boiling point, then leave the thermometer to cool in the water. Before making a syrup, always place the thermometer in hot water to warm. If you put a thermometer straight from the cupboard into hot syrup, it might crack.

PANS
For 'homely' candies that don't demand a perfect appearance, any heatproof container will do as a mold—a casserole or aluminum foil dish, for instance. For more professional results, it's best to use cake pans. Ordinary square or rectangular straight-sided ones are ideal. The size you need will vary according to the quantity made, but 6–8 inch (15–20cm) square pans are probably the most useful. A bigger or smaller pan dimension will simply mean thicker or thinner candies. Whatever the pan, the one thing that is important is that it will help enormously with turning out and cleaning if it is nonstick.

You will also need a wire rack and shallow baking sheet for draining some candies during their production process.

WORK SURFACES
The traditional work surface for candy making is marble, but any heat-absorbent, smooth surface will do—a large baking sheet or a well-oiled heavy wooden cutting board, for example. Avoid pouring very hot syrups directly on to laminated surfaces, as these are not able to withstand such high temperatures, and you are likely to ruin both your candies and your kitchen counter top.

SPATULAS
A wooden spatula is the best tool for working fondants, but flexible metal spatulas are more suitable for turning toffee mixtures and spreading pralines. Keep a selection of both.

BRUSHES
A pastry brush is useful for oiling pans and smaller brushes are ideal decorating tools.

Candy-making equipment, clockwise from top left: heavy saucepans; baking sheets and cake pan; cookie cutters; wire racks; fondant mats; dipping forks; marble work surface; candy thermometer; spatulas and wooden spoons; brushes; heat-resistant bowls.

WRAPPING MATERIALS

There are lots of attractive ways of wrapping candies individually, and the one you choose will probably depend upon whether the sweets are to be given away as a gift or kept to eat at home. The most straightforward choice is to use small squares of wax paper, but clear cellophane or plastic wrap are better options for showing off the gloss and shiny color of candies to full effect. Aluminum foil and metallic wrapping paper, which you can buy in a wide range of colors from stationers and gift stores, can be very attractive. Alternatively, colored cellophane can be used.

The wrapping for square or oblong candies can either be folded over neatly to make a tidy parcel secured with a little tape, or you can twist the two ends in opposite directions, like a traditional toffee wrapper. This method is most suitable for round candies, humbugs or cushion-shaped sweets.

Candies that are not wrapped can be put in small, plain paper candy cases or into pretty decorated or aluminum foil ones. If you are packing two layers of candies into a box, separate the layers with a sheet of wax paper to keep them from sticking to one another.

SCISSORS

You will need a pair of strong, sharp kitchen scissors for cutting toffees and 'pulled' candies. They will need to be oiled before use so that they will cut through cleanly.

METAL CUTTERS

A selection of sharp metal cutters in different shapes and sizes will be useful for making fondants, jellies, and marzipans. Without cutters, you can still make individual sweets, but you will need to cut your candies with a knife into squares or other simple shapes.

DIPPING FORKS

Dipping forks can either have a loop at one end for supporting and scooping out a candy that is being dipped, or two or three prongs for spearing it. Dipping forks can also be used to mark the surface with a pattern or design (see page 34). A carving fork, fondue fork, or ordinary kitchen fork—or even a pair of skewers—can easily be used instead.

FONDANT MAT

A fondant mat is rather like a rubber ice-cube tray except that the indentations are usually a more decorative shape, or sometimes several different shapes. These molds can be used for shaping creams and chocolates, as well as fondants, and may be simple geometric shapes or novelty shapes and characters.

STORAGE CONTAINERS

Unless candies are to be eaten very soon after they have been made, they should be protected from the moisture in the atmosphere to prevent them from becoming sticky.

Caramels, toffees, boiled, and 'pulled' candies must be wrapped individually before being placed in containers, so that they don't stick together, but other types of candy can simply be put carefully into a container that has first been lined with wax paper.

Containers need to be airtight and have no smell that would taint the candies. Glass

A GUIDE TO STORAGE TIMES

Store all candies in a cool, dry place to keep them fresh. Homemade candies will not usually keep for as long as the shop-bought varieties, but in general, the harder the candy, the longer it will keep.

Truffles	2–3 days
Chocolates	10–14 days
Jellies	2 weeks
Nutty candies	2 weeks
Candied and crystallized fruits	6 months
Fudge	3–4 weeks
Caramels	10–14 days
Marzipan, uncooked	1–2 days
Marzipan, unshaped but cooked	3–4 weeks
Marzipan candies, shaped	3 weeks
Boiled candies	3–4 weeks
Nougat	3–4 weeks
Toffees	2 weeks
Fondant, uncooked	Use immediately
Fondant, boiled	6 months

jars show off the natural sparkle and color of candies or their wrappings and make attractive gift containers. If the jar does not have a suitable lid, cover it tightly with aluminum foil, cellophane, or plastic wrap, and secure it firmly with string or sticky tape.

Basic Ingredients

The ingredients list for most candies is very short and simple, and all the important ingredients are in everyday use or readily available. Even the more specialist ingredients are not too difficult to obtain as they are stocked by good food stores or drugstores.

SUGAR
Each different type of sugar gives different characteristics to the candy you are making.

Granulated   This is suitable for most recipes that are heated, but its large crystals will give rather a granular texture to uncooked confections. Use it in **Sugared Apple Jelly** (page 79) or **Barley Sugar Twists** (page 109).

Superfine   This has finer crystals, and dissolves easily, making it more suitable for

Left to right: superfine, light brown, and confectioners' sugar all have different uses.

uncooked pastes. Use this to coat candies, such as **Crystallized Fruit Slices** (page 52).

Confectioners'   This has a very fine texture, ideal for uncooked candies that must be very smooth, such as **Chocolate Peppermint Creams** (page 101). It is also useful sprinkled onto the work surface and rolling pin to prevent mixtures sticking when they are rolled out, and it is sprinkled into pans to line them and onto finished candies to coat them.

Light brown   Fine-grained with moist, clinging crystals that dissolve easily and give a mild, yet distinctive flavor, this sugar is often used for fudge and in the butterscotch of **Nutty Butterscotch Rounds** (page 71).

Dark brown   This sugar is richly flavored and colored, with moist, fine crystals that tend to clump together yet dissolve readily Use this for **Honey and Lemon Toffee** (page 42).

Brown granulated   This has a rich flavor with light golden crystals that remain separate but—as they are large—melt slowly. Because of this, it is best used in mixtures that are

Always use unsalted butter for making candies and dice it before adding to the pan.

boiled to a high temperature, such as toffee. It is delicious in **Pomegranate Chews** (page 69)

Glucose   Available in both powder and syrup form, it is added to candy mixtures to help to control crystallization and make them easier to work. Use it in **Pear Drops** (page 78). It also helps to keep candies made from uncooked fondant soft for longer periods, such as **Strawberry and Raspberry Creams** (page 88). Light corn syrup can be used in place of glucose syrup if necessary.

Honey   Added for the characteristic flavor it will impart to your candies, honey also helps to control crystallization. Use it in **Honeyed Fruit Bars** (page 116).

Corn syrup   This has a mild flavour and, like honey and glucose syrup, helps to keep a mixture smooth by controlling the formation of crystals. Use in **Honey and Hazelnut Caramel** (page 116) or **Honeycomb Toffee** (page119). Golden syrup, a British product, makes a good substitute, if necessary.

FLAVORINGS AND COLORINGS

The recipes in this book rely mostly upon their natural ingredients for flavor and color. This means that your finished sweets may be less vibrant in appearance than the store-bought candies you are used to. If you do wish to add something to boost the flavor of a recipe, look for organic, natural essences, rather than synthetic, artificial flavorings.

So that they will not dilute the syrup, any flavorings that are added must be concentrated and sufficiently strong that only a few drops will be enough to flavor a thick candy mixture.

Similarly, if you feel you want to give a particular sweet a stronger color than its natural ingredients provide, always choose pure vegetable food colorings, rather than synthetic colorings. These are available from good food stores in a wide range of colors. Like flavorings, they are concentrated and need only be used in very small amounts.

BUTTER
Only use good quality, unsalted butter. Always cut the butter into dice before you use it, as this will help to speed up the melting.

CHOCOLATE
Special 'dipping' chocolate or good quality chocolate are the best types to buy for making candies. Using cheap 'cooking' chocolate is a waste of your efforts and produces an inferior candy. For a really rich flavor, use a bittersweet variety of semisweet chocolate.

MILK
Evaporated and condensed milks give more richly flavored candies than fresh milk, as they have been subjected to high temperatures for quite long periods during their processing, and so already have a caramel flavor.

&

Making Sugar Syrup

A sugar syrup is the cornerstone of most candy making, from soft fudges and fondants to hard, boiled sweets. Master this simple technique and you're well on your way to creating a whole range of delicious treats.

Follow these steps as a guide to the techniques you will use, but see the recipes within the rest of this book for the particular ingredients and quantities you need.

USING A CANDY THERMOMETER

• Place your thermometer in hot water to warm up before you start cooking.
• Make sure that the bulb is completely covered by the syrup, but is not touching the bottom of the pan (most thermometers have a casing to help with this).
• As the syrup comes to the boil, check that no sugar crystals are accumulating around the bulb, as this will affect your measurements.
• Always take the reading at eye-level to make it as accurate as possible.

1 Measure the sugar and water into a clean, heavy, deep saucepan that has a capacity of about four times the volume of the ingredients you will be using. Heat gently, stirring with a whisk, until the sugar has dissolved. Stop stirring and allow the syrup to come to boiling point. Stirring at this stage will cause crystals to form and this will give your sweets an unpleasant, grainy texture.

2 Cover the saucepan with a tight-fitting lid so that the steam that condenses on the sides of the pan will wash down any sugar that has begun to crystallize there.

UNDERSTANDING SUGAR

The more sugar there is in a syrup, or the less water, the higher the temperature the solution will boil at. As the syrup continues to boil, more water evaporates, concentrating the syrup further and raising the boiling point higher. The higher the temperature, the harder the candy will set: for instance, the syrup for making toffees is taken to a higher temperature than that for making fudge. To tell what stage has been reached, measure the temperature with a candy thermometer (opposite) or carry out a simple 'water test' (see pages 20–21).

The initial proportions of water and sugar are not critical as it is the final concentration that matters, but if too much water is added at the start of the process it will take longer to reach the required temperature.

When a sugar syrup cools, the sucrose in the sugar will re-form into crystals unless you prevent it. In some candies this crystallization is used in a controlled way—as in the beating of fudges or fondants. For other sweets, where you do not want crystals to form, you can use these anti-crystallizing agents to stop it.

• Acids, such as cream of tartar, lemon juice, or vinegar break down sucrose into other sugars.

• Sugars other than sucrose could be used, such as honey, glucose syrup, or light corn syrup.

• Milks, cream, and butter will thicken a syrup, and hinder the formation of crystals.

3 Another method of removing sugar crystals that form on the side of a saucepan is to use a clean pastry brush, dipped in hot water.

4 Remove the lid after about 3 minutes and put the warmed thermometer in position. Leave the syrup to boil until the correct temperature has been reached, adjusting the heat to maintain a steady boil.

5 If using the testing method (see page 20), remove the pan from the heat and dip the base in cold water to stop the temperature rising any more. Carry out the test. If the right stage has not yet been reached, return the pan to the heat and bring back to the boil for a few more minutes, then dip it in water to stop the cooking and test it again.

Testing the Temperature of Sugar Syrup

If you don't have a candy thermometer, use this method to test what stage of the sugar-boiling process your candies have reached.

Before testing a sugar syrup, always remove the pan from the heat and plunge the base into cold water. This will ensure that the syrup does not continue to get hotter while you work.

A clip is a useful feature of a candy thermometer. It will stop the thermometer slipping into the boiling syrup and will keep the bulb off the base of the pan, so that it is only testing the temperature of the sugar syrup.

Thread stage 223–236°F (106–113°C)
The first setting stage is the thread stage. Drop a teaspoon of syrup onto a cold saucer. When it is cool enough to touch, take a little between your fingers and pull them apart—a thin thread should form between your fingers.

Caramel 320–350°F (160–177°C)
If you boil the syrup beyond this point it will start to burn and your candies will have a bitter taste. Let a little syrup drip off the spoon to check the color. A golden, honey color is a light caramel; a golden amber will make a darker caramel.

Setting Stages

Between the thread stage and caramel, the syrup will gradually get stiffer; the stiffer the syrup, the harder the sweet will be when set.

To test how hard the set will be, drop a small amount of syrup into a bowl of very cold water. Dip your hand in the water and form the syrup into a ball, then compare how it behaves with these five stages.

Soft ball 234–240°F (112–116°C)

The ball flattens when you squeeze it lightly. This is the right stage for fondants and fudge.

Firm ball 244–250°F (118–121°C)

The ball holds its shape when you take it out of the water, but loosens as it warms up. At this stage, the syrup is ready for making caramels.

Hard ball 250–266°F (121–130°C)

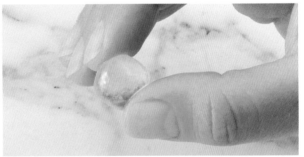

Out of the water, the ball is sticky, but holds its shape under slight pressure. This stage is perfect for nougat and marshmallows.

Soft crack 270–290°F (132–143°C)

Try to pull the ball apart. If it forms threads that are hard, but not brittle, soft crack stage has been reached: perfect for pulled candies.

Hard crack 300–310°F (149–154°C)

If the syrup has hardened in the water and is brittle when you take it out, it has reached the right stage for making hard toffee or rock.

Making Fudge

Once you are confident with making plain fudge, you can begin to experiment with different flavors and ingredients of your own, or try some of the recipes in this book.

The sugar syrup for fudge is boiled to the soft ball stage, then beaten to encourage crystallization of the sugar and give the fudge its characteristic texture and appearance. If you beat the syrup immediately after it has been cooked, you will have firmer candies with a more granular texture. Allow the syrup to cool first if you want a smooth fudge.

Always stir fudge mixtures that have a high milk or cream content to prevent them from sticking in the pan, and be sure to use a large saucepan, as they will boil up considerably.

1 Place your candy thermometer in a bowl of hot water to warm it in preparation for testing the mixture later on. Oil the cake pan you plan to use for setting the fudge.

2 Gently heat the sugar with the milk, cream, or diced butter and any other ingredients according to the recipe, in a heavy saucepan that has a capacity at least four times the volume of the ingredients. Stir with a wooden spoon as you warm the mixture until the sugar has dissolved and any butter or chocolate has melted. Bring to a boil, and boil for 3 minutes.

3 Put the thermometer in the pan, and continue to boil until the required temperature has been reached, stirring if the mixture has a high milk or cream content to prevent it from 'catching'. When the fudge mixture is at soft ball stage (234–240°F/112–116°C), carefully dip the base of the pan in cold water to stop it cooking any more.

4 Beat the mixture immediately with a wooden spoon until it begins to thicken and becomes lighter in color and loses its gloss. For smooth fudge, leave the mixture to cool to about 122°F (50°C), when it is starting to become opaque, then beat until it becomes paler and thickens.

5 Pour the beaten mixture into the oiled pan. Spread the mixture evenly, but do not scrape down the sides of the saucepan to get every last drop of mixture out: these scrapings are likely to have a more grainy texture than your well-beaten fudge and will spoil the end result.

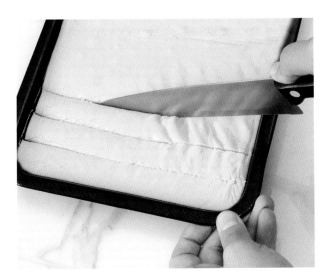

6 Leave the fudge to set until it is firm enough for a line drawn in it with a knife to stay visible, then mark it into squares and leave to set completely.

7 Break or cut the finished fudge into pieces and store it in an airtight container between layers of wax paper. In a cool place, it will keep for 3–4 weeks. Wrapped decoratively, fudge makes a great gift, but make sure it is well sealed to prevent it going stale.

Making Fondant

The creamy, smooth, melting texture of a fondant is achieved through a series of precise stages. Once prepared, fondant can be rolled out and cut into shapes, coated in chocolate, poured into molds, or used to coat fruits.

The steps shown here are for making cooked fondant. Uncooked fondant (page 101) is easier to make, but contains raw egg white, so it is advisable to be cautious and avoid making that for children, the elderly, pregnant women, or other people in an at-risk group.

The first stage in making fondant is to add glucose syrup or corn syrup to a basic sugar syrup (see page 18) to make sure that the sugar crystals formed during the later stages of the process remain small and the fondant is smooth. Glucose syrup keeps the fondant softer for longer than other anti-crystallizing agents, such as cream of tartar or another acid.

The fondant must be cooled quickly and evenly before it is 'worked' to develop the crystallization of the sugar. Finally, to get rid of any lumps, the fondant is kneaded, like a dough for bread. It must then be left for at least 12 hours for the sugar crystals to undergo their final change, which will soften the fondant and give it its creamy, melt-in-the-mouth quality.

This kind of fondant is also used for icing or frosting cakes and for making shaped decorations to go on the cake. It is sometimes known as sugar paste. For decorating, you may wish to add colors to the paste. Do this after your fondant has cured (step 6, opposite): use a toothpick to add dots of natural food coloring to the ball of fondant, then knead until the color is evenly blended. Make sure you color all the fondant you need in one go, as it is very hard to match colors.

1 Start by preparing a sugar syrup, incorporating glucose or corn syrup, to 240°F (116°C), the soft ball stage. When the syrup is nearly ready, sprinkle cold water over a marble slab or other suitable work surface.

2 Dip the base of the saucepan in cold water, then quickly pour the syrup into a pool on the work surface and leave it for a few minutes.

3 Using a dampened metal scraper or large metal spatula, lift the edges of the pool of syrup and fold them to the center. Repeat until the syrup becomes glossy and viscous and has a faint yellow color.

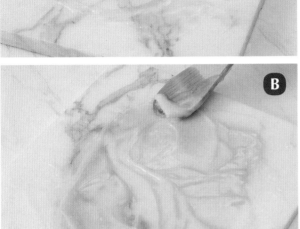

5 With lightly moistened hands, form a ball of fondant, then knead it by pushing half of the ball away from you with the heel of one hand, then folding it back into the lump using a metal scraper or spatula. Repeat in a flowing action for 5–10 minutes until the mixture is free of lumps and feels smooth.

6 Form the fondant into a ball, place it on a dampened plate, cover with a damp cloth to prevent the surface drying out and leave in a cool place to 'cure' for at least 12 hours.

4 Using a damp wooden spatula, work the mixture in a continuous figure of eight action **(A)** for 5–10 minutes **(B)**. Continue until the mixture becomes white and crumbly **(C)** and the stirring is extremely difficult.

7 To roll out fondant, sprinkle the work surface and rolling pin with confectioners' sugar to prevent sticking. Dust cutters with sugar, before and between uses and have a spatula to hand to lift the shapes off the work surface.

Making Caramels

The creamy flavor of caramels is obtained by adding milk, cream, evaporated or condensed milk, and butter; not, as the name suggests, by caramelizing the sugar.

The characteristic chewy texture comes from boiling the syrup to firm ball stage, 244–250°F (118–121°C). You can take the syrup almost up to hard ball range: the hotter the syrup, the firmer the caramel will be.

It is especially important when making caramels to use a large saucepan, because the mixture expands considerably as it boils. Because of their dairy content, caramels are liable to stick to the pan and burn, so use a good, heavy-based pan and stir well as the mixture boils. The thickening effect of the milk helps to prevent the sugar in the syrup from crystallizing, but another anti-crystallizing agent (see page 19) is usually added as well.

1 Brush the base and sides of a cake pan with butter or oil. A wax paper lining can also be used. Place your candy thermometer in a bowl of hot water to warm up.

2 In a large, deep, heavy saucepan, gently heat the sugar with the milk, cream, or diced butter and anti-crystallizing agent. Make sure that the saucepan has a capacity at least four times the volume of the ingredients.

3 Stir the mixture with a wooden spoon until the sugar has dissolved and any butter has melted. Bring to a boil, and boil for about 3 minutes.

4 Put the warmed thermometer into the sugar syrup mixture and continue to boil, stirring gently occasionally and taking care not to knock the thermometer, until the syrup reaches the required temperature.

5 Very carefully, dip the base of the saucepan in cold water to prevent the temperature from rising any further and to stop the caramel from burning as it continues to cook. Quickly, but carefully, pour the caramel into the prepared cake pan and leave it to cool and set.

6 When the caramel is just beginning to set and before it becomes too hard, mark it into pieces with a sharp knife. Oiling the knife helps to prevent it from sticking in the caramel as you work: this will make for a neater job.

7 When the caramel is completely cold and firm, turn it out of the pan, remove the paper from the base if used and cut it into the marked pieces. Wrap each caramel individually in cellophane or wax paper.

Making Pulled Candies

The technique of 'pulling' is used to produce pulled candies, rock, and taffies. It requires strength and stamina—and hands that can withstand high temperatures. It is essential to work the syrup while it is as hot as possible, because it loses pliability as it cools.

Start by boiling a syrup to the hard ball-to-soft crack stage. Allow it to cool until it is just cool enough to handle, then form it into a sausage shape. By repeatedly pulling, folding and twisting the candy, you will incorporate a mass of tiny air bubbles, and give a shiny, silvery appearance to the finished candies.

1 Prepare a syrup to the hard ball-to-soft crack stage (see pages 18–21). When it is nearly ready, lightly oil a marble slab or other suitable surface that will be able to withstand the temperature of the very hot syrup. Do not attempt to make these candies on a laminated work surface—the syrup will be far too hot.

2 Dip the base of the saucepan in cold water to stop the cooking, then pour the syrup quickly into a pool on the prepared work surface. Leave it to cool briefly until a light skin forms on the surface.

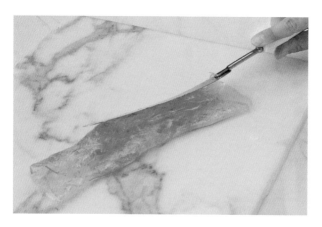

3 Using an oiled metal scraper or large metal spatula, lift the edges of the pool of syrup and fold them into the center. Repeat until the syrup is just cool enough to handle.

4 With oiled hands to prevent sticking, form the syrup into a sausage shape (you may need to use the spatula to help to get you started). Lift up the candy with your hands and pull it out to about 18 inch (45cm) long.

5 Fold it back together and repeat the pulling and folding process until the syrup changes from being soft and slightly sticky to having a firmer, more shiny texture.

6 Fold the pulled syrup in half, twist the two strands together, then pull the twisted sausage out once more until it is about ½ inch (1cm) in diameter.

7 Repeat the folding, twisting, and pulling until the candy becomes opaque, shiny, and is no longer pliable. This may take as long as 20 minutes. Fold in half, then in half again and gently twist the four strands together.

8 Pull out again, gently twisting into a rope, then use oiled, strong scissors to cut the candy into cushion shapes. Wrap these in cellophane or wax paper and store them in an airtight container for 3–4 weeks.

DUAL-COLORED BOILED CANDIES

The 'pulling' technique can also be used to make dual-colored candies. You can combine 'ropes' of two different colored syrups, one pulled until it is opaque, the other left shiny and translucent; or divide a syrup in half and pull one half until it is pale, but leave the other half shiny, then twist the two together.

1 Oil a work surface and prepare a syrup using light brown sugar. Pour the syrup into 2 pools on the work surface. As the edges begin to cool slightly, lift and fold them into the center using an oiled metal scraper or large metal spatula. Keep alternating between pools of syrup to keep both working at the same time.

2 With oiled hands, form 1 pool into a sausage shape, then pull, fold and twist it as you would for normal pulled candy (see previous page). Still with oiled hands, form the second pool

into a sausage, then pull it to a similar length to the first. This time, don't work it so much, so that its color hardly changes.

3 Lay the two pieces side by side, twist them together, then fold the length that is formed over and over to make a short rope.

4 Gently, but firmly and quickly and with a twist at the same time, pull along the length of the rope to produce one long, thin, twisted, but even strand.

5 Using lightly oiled, strong scissors cut the rope into pieces, giving the rope a half turn towards you each time, so that the individual pieces have triangular surfaces. Leave to cool.

6 Store the candies in an airtight container, preferably between layers of wax paper to help to prevent them from sticking.

Working with Chocolate

Many sweets can be dipped or coated in melted chocolate. Follow these steps to make sure that your chocolate is silky smooth, then learn a few techniques overleaf to give your candies a professional, decorated finish.

Always use the best chocolate you can buy. It is not worth spending the time to make candies from cheap brands of chocolate, 'cooking' chocolate sold in unlabelled bags, or chocolate-flavored cake coverings. Special 'dipping' chocolate is available from good confectioners, or use a good quality chocolate. For the most 'chocolatey' flavor, use the least sweetened variety of semisweet chocolate.

MELTING CHOCOLATE

It is vital that chocolate is melted with care; never try to rush this job, or you will ruin the finish of your candies.

1 Chop the chocolate into small pieces so that it will melt quickly and evenly.

2 Place the chocolate in a heat-resistant bowl set over a saucepan of hot, but not boiling, water, making sure the bowl does not touch

KEEP CHOCOLATE DRY

It is especially important when working with chocolate to remember that it will not adhere to a wet or sticky surface, so make sure that any mold to be lined or any ingredient to be coated is completely dry. Make caramels, fondants and marzipans a day in advance to give their outside surface a chance to dry out.

the water. Use a glass bowl so you can see whether the water is bubbling and make sure that the bowl is clear of the water at all times.

3 Remove the saucepan from the heat and stir the chocolate occasionally as it softens until it is free of lumps. Then stir it until it is smooth and liquid. Do not allow the temperature to rise higher than 120°F (49°C), otherwise the flavor of the chocolate will be spoilt.

4 Leave the chocolate to cool and thicken slightly before using it. Once the right coating consistency is reached, keep the temperature constant by putting the bowl over hot water or removing it, as necessary while you work. Throughout the process, make sure that no steam or water gets into the chocolate as it will spoil the candies. Follow this technique for coating fruit, truffles, or fondants in chocolate.

31

DIPPING INTO CHOCOLATE

A dipping fork (see page 15) is a very useful tool for coating candies in chocolate, but it is not essential. Some dipping forks have prongs, like a normal fork, for spearing the item to be coated; others have a hoop at the end, that is used for cradling or scooping the candy you are dipping. To partially coat something, hold it between your thumb and finger or spear it onto a fork or skewer as you dip into the chocolate.

1 Melt the chocolate as described on the previous page. One at a time, place the fruit, soft center, fondant, or whatever you are coating in the chocolate, turn it over gently with a fork, then lift it out on the prongs.

2 Draw the underside of the fork over the rim to remove any drips of chocolate. To partially coat something, spear it on a fork or hold it between thumb and finger and dip just as deep as you want the coating to cover.

3 Gently put the chocolate-coated item onto a tray lined with wax paper and leave it to dry until the chocolate has set hard.

4 Repeat with the remaining sweets or fruits to be coated, keeping a check on the temperature of the chocolate and stirring from time to time to make sure that it does not become too hard. Place the bowl of chocolate back over the hot water to soften it again, if necessary.

MAKING CHOCOLATES IN A MOLD

A fondant mold is a very useful piece of equipment for making soft-centered chocolate candies or chocolates with a nut, piece of fudge, fruit, marzipan or other filling inside. Alternatively, you can make these chocolates in small, aluminum foil candy cases, or even in an ice cube tray: anything that will contain the melted chocolate in a small, bite-size mold. You can use the same technique for making easy chocolate liqueurs, which make a lovely, grown-up gift.

1 Melt the chocolate as described on page 31. One at a time, spoon a little chocolate into each hole of the mold, until it is around one-third full. Tap the mold on your work surface to expel any bubbles of air.

2 Gently tip and rotate the mold to spread the chocolate all round the base and sides. If necessary, use a soft brush to help you to cover the sides evenly, then pour any excess chocolate back into the bowl.

3 Once you have coated each section of the mold, leave the chocolate to set for around 5 minutes. Then add the filling. If it is a soft filling, use the back of a small spoon or your brush to push it gently into all the corners of the mold. Carefully wipe away any filling that is left on the edges of the mold.

4 Make sure the melted chocolate has not started to stiffen while you have been working; place it back over the hot water to loosen again if necessary. Then spoon a little chocolate over each candy to cover the filling. Tap the mold gently on the work surface to eliminate air bubbles and use your brush to smooth the surface and make a good seal around the edges. Leave the candies to set.

DECORATING CHOCOLATES

To give your coated chocolates a professional finish, add a flourish with some simple decorations on the surface. This must be done while the chocolate is still wet.

If you want to add pieces of crystallized fruit or flowers, nuts, or other hard decorations to your candies, put them in place before the chocolate sets completely, so they will stick to the surface.

Parallel lines

Place the back of the prongs of a fork flat on the candy, then lightly draw the fork across the surface of the chocolate or over to one side to make ridges, as shown.

Piping

Fill a wax paper pastry bag with melted chocolate of a contrasting color to the candy, snip off the tip of the bag to leave a very small hole, then pipe fine lines over the candy.

Adding decorations

Fill a wax paper pastry bag with the same melted chocolate used for dipping the candy. Snip off the tip of the bag to leave a very small hole, then pipe a small dot of chocolate onto each candy. Use this as an adhesive to attach a decorative touch, such as a candied flower petal (above) or coffee bean.

Circles

Place the loop end of a dipping fork or similar circular shape, such as the end of a long kebab skewer, on the surface of the candy. Raise it straight upwards slightly, taking threads of chocolate with it to form a circular ridge, then carefully pull the fork straight backwards, towards you, to release it.

Preserving Fruits and Flowers

Candying or crystallizing fruits, flowers, and fruit peels will preserve them, as well as making delicious treats to enjoy. There are a number of different techniques you can use and although the process can take a long time, it requires only a little effort at each different stage.

STORING PRESERVED FRUITS AND FLOWERS

Crystallized confections must be kept dry, or their sugary coating will dissolve, so always pack them in an airtight container between layers of wax paper and keep them in a cool place. Stored carefully, they will keep for up to 6 months.

Candying fruits is a lengthy process that must be done gradually over a number of days—about 14—yet it is very simple to do. Only use fruit that is ripe, but firm, in perfect condition and free from any blemishes.

Small fruits such as cherries, apricots and plums can be left whole but should be pricked all over with a needle to allow the syrup to penetrate the flesh. Larger fruits, such as a pineapple or peaches, should be peeled and cut into pieces. Soft fruits, such as raspberries

and strawberries, are unsuitable, as they will disintegrate during the process.

Glacé fruits are candied fruits that have been dipped in a syrup to give them a glossy finish. See pages 60–61.

Crystallized fruits are candied fruits that have been coated in sugar to give them a crunchy, sugary finish. See page 52.

Most fruits can be candied. The process gives them a lovely, glossy finish.

CANDIED FRUIT

Candying fruit is not just a delicious way of making sweet treats, it also helps to preserve fresh fruit for eating later. Pack the finished candied fruit in boxes, between layers of waxed paper, to keep it fresh, or use it for making glacé or crystallized fruits. Finely chopped, you can use it in baking, too.

1 Prepare the chosen fruit, then poach until just tender. Transfer the fruit to a wire rack placed over a shallow tray to drain while you make a syrup from 1⅓ cups (300ml) of the poaching liquor and ½ cup (125g) sugar.

2 Transfer the fruit that has drained to another shallow tray, then pour over the syrup and leave in a warm place for 24 hours. After 24 hours, move the fruit back to the wire rack to drain again.

3 Increase the concentration of the syrup by dissolving a further ¼ cup (60g) sugar in it, then repeat the process of coating the fruit in syrup, steeping for 24 hours, and draining off the excess 5 more times.

4 Add 6 additional tablespoons of sugar to the syrup. Move the just-drained fruit to the soaking pan, cover with syrup and leave to steep for 48 hours, then repeat the process another time. The longer you leave the fruit for its final steeping phase, the sweeter the finished result will be. Leave for at least 4 days. When you are ready, lift out the fruit, allow it to drain on a wire rack, then put it to dry fully in a warm, dry place. Coat in superfine sugar if desired for effect.

CANDIED PEEL

You can candy and crystallize the peel of citrus fruits: the finished product has a delicious contrast of sweet and sharp flavors. You can even dip the candied peel in chocolate to coat it. To avoid the finished candy having a bitter taint, rinds from citrus fruits should be parboiled before they are crystallized or candied. See page 50 for a recipe for candied peel.

FLOWERS

The crystallizing process for fresh flowers is much quicker than that for fruits, but the initial preparation can be time-consuming, as the entire surface of each petal must be painted evenly with gum Arabic (available from most drugstores).

Small flowers such as violets and rose geraniums can be left whole, but larger ones—shrub roses are the most popular example—are best crystallized when divided into individual petals. They must be in good condition, fresh, and perfectly dry.

1 Using a soft paint brush, coat flower petals with a mixture of gum Arabic and rosewater.

2 Sift superfine sugar over the petals and leave them on a wire rack in a warm place until they are dry and brittle.

Fruit
Candies

ORANGES & LEMONS

CITRUS FRUITS ARE AT THE TOP OF THE LIST OF NATURAL REMEDIES FOR A SORE THROAT OR COMMON COLD, BUT THESE JUICY AND ZINGY FRUITS ARE PACKED WITH OTHER HEALTH BENEFITS, TOO—NOT JUST THE HIT OF VITAMIN C.

Oranges, lemons, limes, and grapefruit contain high levels of powerful antioxidants—including Vitamin C—that offer many health-boosting properties. These can help your immune system to stay strong, ease your stress levels, lower LDL cholesterol and blood pressure, protect bones and joints, and help to prevent osteoporosis. They may also help to ward off serious illnesses, such as cancer, strokes, and heart disease. Some studies have linked Vitamin C with eye function, suggesting that citrus fruit can help to protect eyesight, too.

Much of the goodness in these super fruits is in the peel, which is usually thrown away when you eat the fruit fresh; recipes that use the peel or zest, even in small quantities, will include the health-boosting flavonoids that you might otherwise just discard, including Hesperidin, which can help to lower LDL cholesterol and control blood pressure—so you can feel good about eating these feel-good treats, as long as you indulge yourself in moderation.

Oranges are naturally sweet, but the zesty tang of lemons, limes, and grapefruit lends an invigorating sweet and sour flavor to these tasty homemade treats.

- Chocolate and orange is a classic flavor combination that never fails: try the **White Chocolate Orange Truffles** (page 44) or the **Dark Chocolate Marmalade Bites** (page 47). Even in small quantities, the fruit cuts through the cloying richness of the chocolate, making the sweets a little lighter.

- **Candied Peel** (page 50) makes a delicious, naturally sweet snack and will keep for months in an airtight jar. Of course, you can also use it as an ingredient in other candy recipes, in cakes and other baking, and to decorate homemade citrus candies. Add a decadent twist by dipping candied strips of peel in melted semisweet chocolate (page 50). Small lemons or small oranges, satsumas, or mandarins can be candied whole (page 49) and eaten as they are or sliced to be turned into **Crystallized Fruit Slices** (page 52): a Christmas staple.

- If you're suffering with a cold and an irritating cough, sucking on **Homemade Lemon Sweets** (page 46) will ease your symptoms and is sure to cheer you up. Or you could try some added flavors with cold-busting properties with the **Honey and Lemon Toffee** (page 42) and the **Lemon and Ginger Soft Cheese Fudge** (page 53).

Most citrus fruits are interchangable in recipes as long as you keep the overall quantity of fruit roughly the same. Weigh the fruit to be sure, but as a rough guide, one orange is approximately equivalent to 1½ lemons, 2 limes, or half a grapefruit.

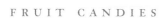

Honey and Lemon Toffee

HONEY AND LEMON ARE A CLASSIC COMBINATION FOR COMBATING THE EFFECTS
OF A COLD. SUCK THESE SQUARES OF TOFFEE AND THE HONEY WILL SOOTHE A SORE
THROAT, WHILE THE HINT OF LEMON WILL HELP TO CLEAR YOUR BLOCKED AIRWAYS.

You will need

- ⅓ cup (75ml) clear honey
- 2 cups (400g) brown sugar
- ¾ cup (170g) unsalted butter, diced
- 1 tablespoon lemon juice

Makes about 1¼lb (550g)

1 Butter or oil a cake pan 8 inch (20cm) square
and warm a candy thermometer in hot water.

2 Gently heat all the ingredients in a heavy
saucepan, stirring with a wooden spoon, until
the sugar has dissolved and the butter melted.

3 Bring to a boil, and boil for 3 minutes.

4 Put the thermometer in the mixture and continue
to boil until the temperature reaches 290°F (143°C),
the soft crack stage.

5 Pour immediately into the prepared cake pan and
leave until just beginning to set.

6 Mark into squares with a lightly oiled, sharp knife
and leave to set completely.

7 Break or cut into pieces. Wrap the pieces
individually in wax paper or cellophane, twisting
the ends together, and store in an airtight container.

Cranberry and Orange Truffles

THESE INDULGENT TRUFFLES ARE BURSTING WITH THE FLAVORS OF THANKSGIVING
AND CHRISTMAS. YOU CAN USE ANY NUTS TO COAT THEM, OR ROLL THEM IN
A DUSTING OF UNSWEETENED COCOA POWDER IF YOU PREFER.

You will need

- 1²/₃ cups (290g) semisweet chocolate pieces
- ²/₃ cup (150ml) heavy cream
- ¹/₃ cup (75ml) Grand Marnier
- Finely grated zest of 1 orange
- 1 cup (100g) finely chopped dried cranberries
- 1 cup (100g) finely chopped walnuts (for coating)

Makes about 35 truffles

1 Soften the chocolate in a heat-resistant bowl placed over a saucepan of hot water.

2 Rinse a second, heavy saucepan with cold water, pour in the cream and bring to a boil.

3 Strain the cream into the chocolate and stir until the chocolate has completely melted and the mixture is smooth.

4 Remove the mixture from the heat and leave to cool to room temperature.

5 Beat in the Grand Marnier, orange zest and cranberry pieces, then cover and chill until the mixture is firm enough to mold.

6 Form the truffles into walnut-sized balls using two cold forks, then roll them in the chopped walnut pieces until they are coated all over.

7 Place in paper cases and chill in the refrigerator until the truffles are firm.

White Chocolate Orange Truffles

POP IN ONE OF THESE TEMPTING TREATS AND IT WILL MELT IN YOUR MOUTH, WITH
THE SUBTLE ZING OF ZESTY ORANGE. IF YOU LIKE, DIP THE TRUFFLES IN MELTED
WHITE OR SEMISWEET CHOCOLATE (PAGE 32) TO GIVE THEM A HARD COATING.

You will need

○ Finely grated zest of 2 oranges
○ ¾ cup (180ml) heavy cream
○ 1½ cups (300g) white chocolate chips
○ ⅓ cup (45g) confectioners' sugar

Makes about 30 truffles

1 Put the cream and orange zest in a small saucepan and heat gently until it starts to simmer. Remove from the heat, cover, and leave to infuse for 30 minutes.

2 Place the chocolate chips in a large bowl, and sit it over a saucepan of simmering water to melt, stirring frequently.

3 Once the chocolate is melted, warm the cream again briefly, then stir into the chocolate until the two are combined.

4 Cover the bowl and leave it to cool, then refrigerate for at least 4 hours, or overnight.

5 Line a baking sheet with aluminum foil or parchment paper, then spoon balls of the chocolate mixture onto it, making each ball about the size of a walnut.

6 Put the sheet of truffles into the freezer for 2 hours. Remove from the freezer, then dust your hands with the confectioners' sugar and roll each truffle gently into a smooth ball. Gently press them back onto the tray to give them a flat base, then return to the freezer for another 2 hours to firm up.

COOK'S NOTES

Don't use the best-quality chocolate that is high in cocoa solids for this recipe – the truffles will set better if you make them with ordinary chocolate chips. Store the truffles in an airtight container in the refrigerator for up to 3 days.

Homemade Lemon Sweets

SUCKING ON ONE OF THESE LITTLE LEMON DROPS WILL SOOTHE A SORE OR TICKLY
THROAT, AND GIVE YOU A BOOST OF VITAMIN C, TOO. CUT THEM INTO ANY SHAPE
YOU LIKE, OR POUR THE LIQUID MIXTURE INTO A SHAPED FONDANT MOLD.

You will need

- 2½ cups (580ml) unsweetened apple purée
- 1½ cups (350g) sugar
- ⅓ cup (75ml) water
- 1½oz (40g) powdered gelatin
- A few drops of lemon extract
- Cornstarch and confectioners' sugar, for dusting

Makes about 1lb (500g)

1 Rinse a baking pan with cold water to wet it.

2 Heat the apple purée and sugar in a heavy-based
saucepan and slowly bring to the boil, stirring.
Cook steadily until the mixture is very thick, then
remove the pan from the heat.

3 Put the water in a small bowl and sprinkle over
the powdered gelatin. Stand the bowl in another
bowl of hot water and stir until the gelatin dissolves.

4 Stir the gelatin into the apple mixture with the
lemon extract.

5 Pour the liquid into the damp pan and leave to
set in a cool place for at least 6 hours.

6 Turn out the set jelly onto a cold work surface to
cut. Use a sharp, wet knife to cut into squares or
diamonds, or use small, shaped cookie cutters to
make circles or any other shape you like. Dust the
finished candies with a mixture of cornstarch and
confectioners' sugar.

Dark Chocolate Marmalade Bites

ONE OF THESE RICH CHOCOLATE BITES GOES A LONG WAY: STUDIES HAVE SHOWN THAT EATING A SMALL AMOUNT OF SEMISWEET CHOCOLATE TWO OR THREE TIMES A WEEK MAY EVEN HELP TO LOWER YOUR BLOOD PRESSURE. THEY MAKE FABULOUS GIFTS, TOO.

You will need

○ 6 oranges
○ 5 cups (1.15kg) sugar
○ 2 cups (350g) broken or chopped semisweet chocolate
○ Chocolate bar mold

Makes 16

1 Start by making the marmalade filling. Finely chop the oranges to the coarseness you prefer (using a food processor is the quickest way to do this, if you have one). If you do not want much orange rind in your marmalade, partially peel the oranges before chopping.

2 Place the prepared oranges in a heavy saucepan with the sugar and bring to a boil. Keep the mixture at a rolling boil for 20 minutes, until it begins to thicken. Remove from the heat.

3 Carefully pour into cleaned and sterilized jars, seal and leave to cool. For this recipe, you will need only about ½ cup marmalade; the rest will keep for up to a year in a cool place.

4 Once the marmalade is cool, you can assemble the chocolates. Melt two-thirds of the chocolate (see page 31) then add the remaining pieces of chocolate and stir briskly until it is fully melted. Pour just enough chocolate into the chocolate bar mold to cover the base.

5 Gently spoon on a thin line of marmalade, making sure that the fruit does not reach the top of the mold or touch the sides. Spoon on melted chocolate to completely surround the marmalade. Gently tap the mold on the counter to remove any air bubbles.

6 Leave to cool until the chocolate has set, then turn the candies out of the mold. Store in an airtight container in a cool place for up to 2 weeks.

COOK'S NOTES

Try using different citrus fruit in your marmalade, but keep the overall quantity as close to the recipe as you can. You'll need to substitute 2 limes or 1½ lemons for 1 orange. You can make these chocolate bars with store-bought marmalade, as long as it has a thick consistency: you will need about ½ cup.

Candied Oranges and Lemons

MAKING CANDIED FRUIT IS A SIMPLE, BUT LENGTHY PROCESS; BUT THE RESULTS
ARE MELT-IN-THE-MOUTH SWEET AND DELICIOUS. YOU CAN EAT THE CANDIED FRUITS
AS THEY ARE, OR TURN THEM INTO CRYSTALLIZED OR GLACÉ FRUITS INSTEAD.

You will need

○ 1lb (450g) prepared fresh fruit
○ Approximately 1½lb (680g) sugar

Makes about 1lb (450g)

1 Gently poach the fruit in a heavy saucepan in just enough water to cover it until just tender: small or soft pieces will only take 2–4 minutes; larger, firmer ones will need 10–15 minutes. Transfer the fruit to a wire rack placed over a tray and leave it to drain.

2 Measure 1¼ cups (280ml) of the poaching liquid, add ¾ cup (140g) sugar and heat gently, stirring with a wooden spoon, until the sugar has dissolved. Bring to a boil.

3 Arrange the fruit in a single layer in a shallow dish and pour over the boiling syrup. If there is not enough syrup to cover the fruit, prepare some more by dissolving 1 cup (190g) sugar in 1 cup (225ml) water.

4 Cover the fruit with wax paper to keep it completely submerged and leave it in a warm place to steep for 24 hours.

5 Using a slotted spoon, transfer the fruit to a wire rack placed over a tray and leave to drain.

6 Pour the soaking syrup into a saucepan, add ¼ cup (50g) sugar and heat gently, stirring with a wooden spoon, until the sugar has dissolved. Bring the syrup to a boil.

7 Return the fruit to the shallow dish, pour the syrup over, cover with wax paper and leave in a warm place for another 24 hours.

8 Repeat steps 5, 6 and 7 five times more. Then repeat step 5, then step 6 using 6 tablespoons sugar. Repeat step 7, but this time leave the fruit to soak for 48 hours instead of 24.

9 Lift out the fruit and make another syrup with 6 tablespoons sugar, then return the fruit to the shallow dish, pour over the syrup, cover and leave for at least 4 days. Then, using a slotted spoon, transfer the fruit to a wire rack placed over a tray and leave to drain for one last time.

10 Leave the fruit in a warm place, such as an airing cupboard or over a radiator, until it is completely dry.

11 Pack into cardboard or wooden boxes between layers of waxed paper, or use for crystallized or glacé fruits (pages 53 and 60).

COOK'S NOTES

The longer you leave the fruit in the syrup for its final steeping phase (step 9, above), the sweeter the finished candied fruit will be.

Candied Peel

HERE'S A SWEET TREAT THAT IS POSITIVELY GOOD FOR YOU: THE ZEST OF ORANGES AND OTHER CITRUS FRUITS CONTAINS CONCENTRATED GOODNESS THAT IS OFTEN JUST PEELED OFF AND THROWN AWAY.

You will need

○ 5 small oranges, 2 lemons or 2 small grapefruit
○ 1½ cups (350g) sugar

1 Scrub the fruit, cut it into halves or quarters and scrape away all the flesh, leaving the peel intact.

2 In a saucepan, simmer the peel, just covered by water, for 1½–2 hours until tender, topping up with fresh water as necessary. Change the water two or three times when cooking grapefruit peel.

3 Remove the peel from the liquid with a slotted spoon and lay it on a wire rack placed over a tray to allow the liquid to drain off. Reserve the cooking liquor.

4 Measure 1¼ cups (280ml) of the cooking liquor into a heavy saucepan; add extra water if necessary. Add 1 cup (190g) sugar and heat gently, stirring, until the sugar has dissolved. Bring to a boil, add the peel, return to a boil, then remove from the heat, cover, and leave in a warm place for 2 days.

5 Using a slotted spoon, transfer the peel to a wire rack placed over a tray and allow to drain. Add the remaining sugar to the syrup, heat gently, stirring, until the sugar has dissolved. Return the peel to the saucepan, bring to a boil, then simmer until the peel is transparent. Remove from the heat.

6 Once cool, transfer the peel and syrup to an airtight container and leave for 2–3 weeks, then lift out with a slotted spoon and transfer to a wire rack over a tray to drain. Leave it in a warm place to dry completely, then store in airtight, sterilized jars.

COOK'S NOTES

You can make delicious treats by dipping candied peel in melted chocolate to coat it. Candy the peel in thin strips, then half dip them in chocolate or coat completely. Lay the pieces on wax paper until the chocolate sets.

ACTIVELY GOOD

ORANGE PEEL OFTEN GETS DISCARDED, BUT THE ZEST USED IN THIS RECIPE CONTAINS A FLAVONOID CALLED HESPERIDIN, WHICH CAN HELP TO LOWER LDL CHOLESTEROL AND CONTROL BLOOD PRESSURE.

Crystallized Fruit Slices

WITH THEIR COMBINATION OF SUGAR AND SHARPNESS, CITRUS FRUITS
ARE PARTICULARLY GOOD WHEN MADE INTO CRYSTALLIZED FRUIT BITES.
START BY CANDYING SLICES OF FRUIT, THEN GIVE THEM THIS SUGARY FINISH.

You will need

○ Superfine sugar
○ Candied fruits (page 49)

1 Bring a saucepan of water to a boil, and put plenty of superfine sugar into a bowl.

2 Slice the candied fruits, then spear one piece at a time on a dipping fork or a skewer. Dip it in the boiling water, allow the excess moisture to drain off, then roll the fruit in the sugar to coat it well and evenly. Press the sugar on lightly so that it does not all fall off when you pick up the fruit.

3 Place the fruit slices on a wire rack and leave them to dry in a warm place. Keep them in an airtight container to preserve the sugary finish.

ACTIVELY GOOD

VITAMIN C IS NOT JUST GOOD FOR WARDING OFF COLDS. IT ALSO HELPS THE BODY TO MAKE COLLAGEN, WHICH BUILDS BODY TISSUE. THIS MEANS THAT A GOOD VITAMIN C INTAKE IS ESSENTIAL FOR STRONG SKIN, TEETH, LIGAMENTS, AND TENDONS, AND WILL ENCOURAGE WOUNDS TO HEAL.

Lemon and Ginger Soft Cheese Fudge

SOFT CHEESE MAKES A REALLY CREAMY FUDGE. IT DOESN'T KEEP FOR LONG, BUT
MAKE A BATCH IF YOU FEEL A COLD STARTING: GINGER HAS ANTI-INFLAMMATORY
AND ANTISEPTIC PROPERTIES THAT CAN HELP TO STOP COUGHS AND EASE COLDS.

You will need

- 2 cups (350g) semisweet chocolate, chopped
- 1/3 cup (75g) low-fat soft cheese
- 2 cups (275g) confectioners' sugar, sifted
- 1 small lemon, peeled and chopped
- 1/4 cup (50g) candied ginger, chopped
- Small pieces of lemon and candied ginger, to decorate

Makes 36

1 Line a shallow 10 x 8 inch (25 x 20cm) cake pan with wax paper.

2 Place the chocolate in a small, heat-resistant bowl over a pan of hot water, and stir occasionally until melted (see page 31) then remove from the heat.

3 Place the soft cheese in a separate bowl then gradually beat in the melted chocolate and then the confectioners' sugar a little at a time.

4 Stir the lemon and ginger into the fudge, then spoon into the prepared pan. Refrigerate until firm.

5 Cut out shapes or squares of fudge, and decorate with lemon and ginger pieces. Keep refrigerated in an airtight container with wax paper between layers, and eat within 7 days.

COOK'S NOTES

This fudge tastes delicious when it is made with orange, too. Just substitute one satsuma for the lemon in the recipe.
A serrated knife is the best choice for slicing the flesh of citrus fruits. A bread knife will do, but if you have a smaller tomato knife you will find it easier to use.

EXOTIC FRUITS

THE FRUITS AND NUTS IN THE RECIPES WITHIN THIS SECTION ARE MOSTLY GROWN IN HOT, SUNNY REGIONS, BUT WHEREVER YOU LIVE, YOU'LL FIND THEM IN GOOD GROCERY STORES AND CAN USE THEM TO ADD AN EXOTIC TOUCH TO YOUR CANDIES.

Many of these fruits are most easily available in dried form, but when eaten like this, they will have lost some of their health-giving benefits. When you are buying dried fruits, read the packaging and take care to avoid products that include added sulfites, if you can. These are sometimes added during the drying process as a preservative, but they can trigger breathing difficulties in asthmatics and other people with a sulfite sensitivity.

- If you have digestive problems—not just constipation, but other intestinal ailments, too—fiber-rich figs and dates can often offer relief. You can stuff them with marzipan (page 64) or dip them in chocolate (page 75) as an occasional treat.

- The high levels of potassium in figs may also help to lower blood pressure; try **Double-dip Chocolate Fruit** (page 58), or a variation on the decadent **Chocolate-stuffed Prunes** (page 75) to get more figs into your diet and treat yourself at the same time.

- **Marzipan-stuffed Apricots** (page 65) are packed not just with marzipan, but with heart-healthy beta-carotene, which studies have shown can help to combat LDL cholesterol—the so-called

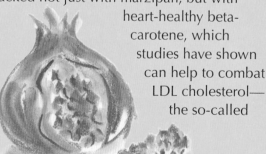

'bad cholesterol' that can cause arteries to block or blood clots to form.

- Many of these fruits used in this section pair perfectly with carob, a caffeine-free chocolate substitute with myriad health benefits. See **Tropical Delights** (page 70) to find out more about the ways that carob can help to combat health problems.

- **Chocolate-coated Cape Gooseberries** (page 56)—fruits that are also known as Physalis—will give a hit of polysaccharides, which may help to strengthen your immune system, and, like kumquats (see **Candied Kumquats**, page 61), are high in vitamin C.

- You can use almost any small fruit for the **Double-dip Chocolate Fruit** (page 58) and **Fondant-dipped Fruits** (page 59), and if they have stalks attached it's even easier to do. Cherries are perfect, and you'll benefit from their anti-inflammatory properties, which can help to ease the symptoms of arthritis and gout, and soothe aching joints and muscles after exercise.

- Nuts and seeds offer a range of essential nutrients and may help to boost your brain power and mood with their high levels of omega-3 fatty acids. Many contain an amino acid called tryptophan, which the body can convert into serotonin—a natural cure for insomnia and mild cases of depression. Scatter a handful of brain food on **Tropical Delights** (page 70) and **Nutty Butterscotch Rounds** (page 71).

Chocolate-coated Cape Gooseberries

MOST FRUITS AND NUTS CAN BE DIPPED IN MELTED CHOCOLATE. CAPE
GOOSEBERRIES, OR PHYSALIS, WITH THEIR STALKS STILL ATTACHED HAVE A BUILT-IN
HANDLE FOR EASY DIPPING AND GIVE A PARTICULARLY ATTRACTIVE RESULT.

You will need

- ⅔ cup (110g) white chocolate pieces
- ⅔ cup (110g) semisweet chocolate pieces
- 24 Cape gooseberries

Makes 24 coated fruits

1 Melt the white chocolate over a hot water bath,
as described on page 31, then remove the bowl
from the heat. Stir the melted chocolate well to
ensure that it is smooth and a good consistency for
dipping and coating the fruit.

2 One by one, hold the fruits by their stems and dip
them into the melted chocolate. You can dip them
right up to the stem, or just part way, but for the
best finished result, try to be consistent.

3 Lift the fruit out of the chocolate and allow any
excess to drip back into the bowl, then carefully
transfer the coated fruit to wax paper and leave to
dry. Coat half the fruits with white chocolate, then
repeat the process with the semisweet chocolate
and the remaining fruits.

4 To store the chocolate-dipped fruits, place them
in small paper candy cases, then arrange in a single
layer in a candy box or other airtight container and
keep in a cool place.

> ### ACTIVELY GOOD
> WEIGHT-FOR-WEIGHT, CAPE GOOSEBERRIES
> CONTAIN TWICE AS MUCH VITAMIN C
> AS LEMONS. THEY ARE ALSO HIGH IN
> POLYSACCHARIDES, WHICH MAY HELP TO
> STRENGTHEN THE IMMUNE SYSTEM.

Double-dip Chocolate Fruit

THE CONTRAST OF WHITE AND SEMISWEET CHOCOLATE ON THESE TWICE-DIPPED
BEAUTIES IS STRIKINGLY ATTRACTIVE. TAKE YOUR TIME TO DO A NEAT JOB AND
GIVE THE WHITE CHOCOLATE TIME TO SET PROPERLY BEFORE DIPPING INTO
THE DARK, OR YOU WILL END UP WITH A MESSY FINISHED PRODUCT.

You will need

○ Around 12 pieces of fresh fruit, such as
strawberries, cherries, orange segments, kiwi fruit,
or stoned dried fruits (dates, apricots, or prunes)
○ 1 cup (175g) good quality white chocolate
○ 1/2 cup (75g) semisweet chocolate

Makes 12 pieces of dipped fruit

1 Clean and prepare the fruit. Wipe strawberries
with a soft cloth or pastry brush; wash and dry
firm-skinned fruits; peel or slice other fruits as
necessary. Lay the fruit on paper towels to absorb
any remaining moisture.

2 Chop or break the chocolate into bite-size pieces.
Set a heat-resistant bowl over a pan of simmering
water and add the white chocolate. Melt the
chocolate (see page 31), stirring frequently until it
is smooth, then remove the bowl from the heat.

3 Leave the chocolate to cool until it is tepid,
stirring from time to time to keep it smooth.

4 Line a baking sheet with wax paper or aluminum
foil, then start to dip the fruit into the chocolate.
Hold each piece by its stem or one end and dip it
at an angle, covering about two-thirds of the fruit.

5 Allow the excess chocolate to drip off, then lay
each piece of fruit on the lined baking sheet to set.

6 If the chocolate starts to thicken up, put the bowl
back over the simmering water for a short while to
soften it slightly once more.

7 Using a clean heat-resistant bowl, melt the
semisweet chocolate in the same way as the white.
Once it is smooth and silky, remove it from the heat
and allow to cool until it is tepid.

8 Take the pieces of fruit and dip them in the
melted chocolate at the opposite angle to before,
to create a chevron effect. Lay them back on the
baking sheet and refrigerate until the chocolate
has set.

Fondant-dipped Fruits

YOU CAN LOOSEN A FONDANT MIXTURE BY MELTING IT OVER A HOT WATER BATH UNTIL
IT IS THE RIGHT CONSISTENCY FOR DIPPING AND COATING FRUITS OR NUTS.
ONCE THE FONDANT HAS DRIED, YOU COULD DIP THESE SWEET TREATS AGAIN,
THIS TIME IN MELTED CHOCOLATE FOR A DOUBLE-DIP DELIGHT.

You will need

○ 2 cups (380g) sugar
○ 2/3 cup (140ml) water
○ 1 tablespoon glucose syrup or corn syrup
○ About 1lb (450g) small whole fruit, such as strawberries, grapes, cherries, or Cape gooseberries with stems, or perfect segments of tangerines.

Makes about 1lb (450g)

1 Prepare the fondant using the sugar and water as described on page 24, incorporating the glucose or corn syrup into the sugar syrup, then allow the fondant to 'cure' overnight.

2 Wash the fruit and dry it well, discarding any fruits that are less than perfect.

3 Melt the fondant in a heat-resistant bowl placed over a saucepan of hot water, stirring constantly, and adding a little hot water if it is too thick to give an even coating. Do not let the temperature exceed 150°F (65°C)—it must not start to boil.

4 Holding each piece of fruit by its stem, or by one end, carefully dip the fruit into the melted fondant.

5 Allow any excess fondant to drain back into the bowl, then carefully lay the fruit on wax paper and leave to dry for 5–10 minutes.

6 Once the fondant has set, place the fruits in small paper candy cases to prevent them from sticking together and to make an attractive presentation if they are a gift.

ACTIVELY GOOD

CHERRIES WORK WELL WITH THIS RECIPE AND HAVE EXCELLENT ANTI-INFLAMMATORY PROPERTIES THAT CAN HELP TO EASE THE SYMPTOMS OF GOUT AND ARTHRITIS. SOME STUDIES CLAIM THAT THEY CAN HELP TO LESSEN ACHING MUSCLES AND JOINT PAIN AFTER EXERCISE, MAKING THESE CANDIES THE PERFECT POST-WORKOUT TREAT.

COOK'S NOTES

If your fondant is too stiff or your fruits too ripe, the fruits may fall off their stems or stalks as you dip them. Add a little more hot water to the fondant to loosen it if necessary. Alternatively, carefully hold the fruits with a pair of ice tongs and part-dip them instead, if you find dipping by the stalks is not working.

Glacé Fruits

CANDIED, OR GLACÉ CHERRIES MAY NOT BE ABLE TO SHAKE OFF THEIR GARISHLY
KITSCH IMAGE, BUT THEY ARE SWEET, STICKY, AND SECRETLY MORISH. ANY FRUIT
THAT CAN BE CANDIED (PAGE 49) CAN ALSO BE TURNED INTO GLACÉ FRUIT.

You will need

- 2 cups (380g) sugar
- 2/3 cup (150ml) water
- 1lb (450g) candied fruit (page 49)

Makes about 1lb (450g)

1 Gently heat the sugar in the water, stirring with a wooden spoon until the sugar has dissolved.

2 Bring the syrup to a boil and boil for 1 minute. At the same time, bring a separate saucepan of water to a boil.

3 Remove the syrup from the heat. Pour a little into a cup and cover the rest to keep it warm.

4 Spear one piece of fruit at a time on a dipping fork or skewer. Dip the fruit into the saucepan of boiling water, allow the excess water to drain off, then dip the fruit into the syrup in the cup.

5 Leave the fruit on a wire rack to drain.

6 As the syrup in the cup becomes cloudy, replace it with fresh syrup from the saucepan.

7 Turn the pieces of fruit over occasionally to ensure that they dry evenly.

Candied Pineapple Bites

PINEAPPLE CHUNKS MAKE DELICIOUS MORSELS OF SWEETNESS. THE ANTI-OXIDANT PROPERTIES OF THE FRUIT'S ABUNDANT VITAMIN C CAN HELP TO EASE AND PREVENT THE SYMPTOMS OF HEART DISEASE, OSTEOARTHRITIS, AND RHEUMATOID ARTHRITIS.

You will need

○ 1 whole pineapple
○ 2 cups (380g) sugar
○ 1 cup (225ml) water

Makes about 1 1/2 lb (700g)

1 Peel and core the pineapple and cut the flesh into bite-size pieces.

2 Make a sugar syrup (see page 18) by heating the sugar and water together in a heavy saucepan.

3 When the syrup comes to a boil, add the pineapple pieces and reduce the heat. Simmer until the fruit begins to look translucent.

4 Remove the pan from the heat. Use a slotted spoon to remove the fruit from the syrup and put it to drain on a wire rack. You can allow the fruit to dry fully at this stage, but for a sweeter and more intense candied flavor, follow the sequence of steeping, draining, and steeping again in the syrup as described on page 49.

Candied Kumquats

THIS PERSIAN CITRUS IS SHARP WHEN FRESH, BUT—CANDIED—IT'S DELICIOUS POPPED WHOLE INTO YOUR MOUTH. ADD SOME SPICE TO THE CANDYING SYRUP FOR EXTRA DEPTH—A FEW STAR ANISE OR A CINNAMON STICK ARE IDEAL.

You will need

○ 1 1/2 cups (350g) sugar
○ 1 cup (225ml) water
○ 3 cups (450g) kumquats
○ Star anise or cinnamon stick, optional

Makes about 3 cups (450g)

1 Make a syrup with the sugar and water. Bring it to a boil in a heavy saucepan, then add the kumquats and any spices or other flavorings you want to use.

2 Simmer, uncovered, for 10–15 minutes, until the fruit is just tender when pierced with a knife.

3 Remove the pan from the heat and allow the fruit to steep in the syrup for 4 hours.

4 Strain and reserve the fruit, then return the syrup to the pan and boil for around 10 minutes, until it is thick enough to coat the back of a spoon.

5 Place the kumquats in a large, sterilized jar and pour over the thickened syrup. Seal the jar.

6 If you prefer, dry the candied kumquats on a wire rack in a warm place, such as an airing cupboard, until they are no longer sticky to touch.

Marzipan

TRADITIONALLY MARZIPAN IS MADE FROM GROUND ALMONDS, BUT OTHER NUTS WILL MAKE DIFFERENT VARIATIONS. ONCE YOU ARE CONFIDENT MAKING BASIC MARZIPAN, EXPERIMENT BY COATING PIECES WITH MELTED CHOCOLATE, OR USING THE MARZIPAN TO STUFF DRIED FRUITS (PAGES 64–65).

Uncooked Marzipan

You will need

- Scant 1 cup (130g) confectioners' sugar, sifted
- ½ cup (100g) superfine sugar
- 2 cups (170g) ground almonds
- 1 teaspoon lemon juice
- 2 egg yolks, beaten

Makes about 1lb (450g)

1 Mix the sugars together in a bowl and stir in the ground almonds.

2 Add the lemon juice and sufficient egg yolks to give a stiff consistency.

3 Form the marzipan into a ball and knead it lightly until it is smooth. Don't overknead the marzipan, or it will start to become greasy. If the paste seems too wet, sprinkle on some more confectioners' sugar and work it in by kneading.

4 Use the marzipan immediately if required or wrap it in wax paper or plastic wrap and store in an airtight container in a cool place. It will keep for up to a week in the refrigerator.

COOK'S NOTES

There are two types of marzipan—cooked and uncooked. Cooked (boiled) marzipan (opposite) is based on a boiled sugar syrup, and is a little softer to work with, so is the one to choose for making marzipan novelties. Uncooked marzipan contains raw egg yolks, so avoid this type for children, pregnant women, the elderly, or other people in an at-risk group.

Boiled Marzipan

You will need

○ Confectioners' sugar, for dusting
○ 2 cups (380g) sugar
○ $^2/_3$ cup (150ml) water
○ A pinch of cream of tartar
○ 4 cups (340g) ground almonds
○ 2 egg whites, lightly beaten

Makes about 2lb (900g)

1 Sprinkle confectioners' sugar over a marble surface or a large baking sheet and put your candy thermometer in a bowl of hot water to warm.

2 Gently heat the sugar in the water in a heavy saucepan, stirring with a wooden spoon until the sugar has dissolved.

3 Add the cream of tartar and bring to a boil for 3 minutes.

4 Place the candy thermometer in the saucepan and continue to boil until the temperature of the syrup reaches 240°F (116ºC), the soft ball stage (see page 21).

5 Remove the pan from the heat and dip the base of the saucepan in cold water, then beat the syrup until the mixture becomes thick and creamy.

6 Stir in the ground almonds, then the egg whites until well combined.

7 Place the saucepan over a low heat and stir thoroughly for about 2 minutes, until the marzipan mixture thickens.

8 Turn the marzipan onto the work surface or baking sheet and begin to work it with a metal spatula until it is cold enough to handle, then knead it with your hands lightly dusted with confectioners' sugar until it is smooth and pliable.

9 Use as required or wrap in wax paper, place in an airtight container, and store in a cool place.

Marzipan-stuffed Dates

DATES ARE WELL-KNOWN AS A REMEDY FOR CONSTIPATION, BUT THEY ARE
ALSO HIGH IN IRON, AND CONTAIN A RANGE OF ELEMENTS THAT ARE ESSENTIAL
TO BONE HEALTH. BECAUSE THEY ARE PACKED WITH NATURAL SUGARS,
THEY MAKE A GREAT, ENERGY-BOOSTING SNACK.

You will need

○ 24 dates
○ 6oz (175g) marzipan (see pages 62–63)
○ Superfine sugar for dusting

Makes 24

1 Select good quality dates. Cheaper ones will be smaller and probably drier, and not so delicious.

2 With a small, sharp knife, slit along the length of each date and carefully lift out the pit.

3 Form the marzipan into small pieces that will fit into the cavities left by the pits.

4 Fill the dates with the marzipan, roll them in superfine sugar, then put them in small paper candy cases and leave to dry.

COOK'S NOTES

If you want to color your marzipan like the filling shown here (left), add a few drops of natural food coloring when you add the ground almonds to a boiled marzipan recipe (page 63), or when you add the egg yolks for uncooked marzipan (page 62). You can also add flavorings at this stage, such as chocolate. Add 1/3 cup (50g) chocolate, melted and mixed with a tablespoon of hot water, for each 1lb (450g) marzipan you are making.

Marzipan-stuffed Apricots

HIGH IN FIBER AND BETA-CAROTENE, APRICOTS CAN HELP TO PROTECT YOUR
HEART, DIGESTIVE SYSTEM, AND EYESIGHT. WHEN BUYING DRIED APRICOTS,
CHECK THE PACKET AND TRY TO AVOID ANY THAT HAVE BEEN TREATED WITH
SULFITES DURING THE DRYING PROCESS OR TO EXTEND THEIR SHELF LIFE.

You will need

○ 24 dried apricots
○ 6oz (175g) marzipan (see pages 62–63)
○ 1½ cups (270g) semisweet chocolate pieces

Makes 24

1 Soak the dried apricots in water overnight until
they are plump, then poach them lightly in their
soaking water in a saucepan until they are just
tender. You can omit this stage if you have the type
of apricot that requires no soaking, though these
usually contain sulfites (see above).

2 Strain off the poaching water and spread the
apricots on a wire rack to drain off any excess
liquid, then pat them dry.

3 Use a small, sharp knife to slit along the length
of each apricot and open out the flesh.

4 Form the marzipan into small pieces that will
just fit inside the cavities and carefully stuff the
marzipan inside the fruits.

5 Melt the chocolate pieces (see page 31) over a
hot water bath, stirring until it is completely melted
and smooth, then remove the bowl from the heat.

6 One by one, half-dip the stuffed apricots into
the melted chocolate. Allow any excess chocolate
to drip back into the bowl, then lay the fruits on a
baking sheet lined with parchment paper and leave
until the chocolate has set. If the chocolate in the
bowl starts to stiffen up, return it to the heat over
simmering water until it is smooth again.

Quince Jellies

QUINCES ARE SELDOM FOUND IN THE SUPERMARKET, BUT IF YOU ARE LUCKY
ENOUGH TO HAVE A BUSH OR TREE IN THE GARDEN, OR FIND SOME AT A LOCAL
MARKET, THEIR FRAGRANT FLAVOR MAKES A DELICIOUSLY UNUSUAL SWEET TREAT.

You will need

- 3lb (1.3kg) quinces, peeled, cored and sliced
- 1 cup (225ml) water
- Sugar, see step 3 below, plus extra for coating

Makes about ½lb (250g)

1 Put the quinces and water in a heavy saucepan and bring to a boil. Cook gently until the fruit is tender and pink—about 1½ hours, depending on the ripeness of the fruit.

2 Remove the pan from the heat. Without straining the fruit, mash it to a soft purée and then push it through a strainer so that it is smooth.

3 Weigh the purée and return it to the pan with the same weight of sugar. Stir over a low heat until the sugar has dissolved completely, then increase the heat and cook, stirring all the time so that the mixture does not stick or burn.

4 Heat the oven to its lowest setting and line several baking sheets with parchment paper.

5 When the mixture is very thick and leaves the sides of the pan as you stir, remove the pan from the heat and spread out the purée to a depth of ½ inch (1cm) thick on the prepared baking sheets. Let the mixture cool slightly, then use wet hands to lightly press and smooth it.

6 Place the baking sheets in the oven, leave the door ajar and leave to dry out for about 12 hours.

7 Remove from the oven and allow to cool. Cut the finished jelly into squares with a hot, sharp knife and roll them in sugar to coat all over. Pack into an airtight container between layers of parchment paper and store in a cool dry place.

Pineapple Marzipan Roll

ONCE YOU HAVE MASTERED THE BASIC TECHNIQUE OF THIS MARZIPAN ROLL,
EXPERIMENT WITH FLAVOR COMBINATIONS BY KNEADING A LITTLE COFFEE ESSENCE
OR CHOCOLATE SAUCE INTO THE MARZIPAN, OR USING DIFFERENT CANDIED FRUIT.

You will need

○ 10oz (280g) boiled marzipan (page 62)
○ Confectioners' sugar for rolling out
○ ½ cup (60g) glace pineapple pieces (page 60)
○ Superfine sugar, for dusting

Makes about 24

1 Knead the marzipan on a surface lightly dusted with confectioners' sugar until it is soft and pliable.

2 Roll it out to a thickness of ¼ inch (5mm), in as neat a rectangle as you can.

3 Finely chop the pineapple pieces, then scatter them evenly over the sheet of marzipan.

4 Starting with one of the longest edges, roll up the marzipan, pressing it gently but firmly into shape. Cut the marzipan into strips first if you find it hard to manage a wide roll.

5 Dust your work surface with superfine sugar and roll the finished marzipan log in it to coat the outer surface evenly all over.

6 Use a sharp knife to cut the marzipan log into bite-size, pinwheel rounds.

Pomegranate Chews

LOOK FOR POMEGRANATE MOLASSES IN HEALTH FOOD STORES, OR
LEBANESE OR MIDDLE EASTERN GROCERIES. IT IS THICK, STICKY AND
TART, AND ADDS AN EXOTIC FLAVOR TO THESE CHEWY, CARAMEL SWEETS.

You will need

○ 1¼ cups (250g) granulated sugar
○ ¼ cup (60ml) water
○ 1 tablespoon light corn syrup
○ 3 tablespoons pomegranate molasses
○ ½ cup (115g) butter

Makes about 1lb (450g)

1 Grease a 9 inch (23cm) cake pan or line it with aluminum foil and put your candy thermometer in a bowl of hot water to warm up.

2 Put all the ingredients in a heavy saucepan over a medium heat and stir until everything is dissolved and well combined.

3 Put the candy thermometer into the mixture and bring it to the boil. Stir the mixture regularly to make sure that it does not stick or burn on the bottom of the pan, and boil until the mixture reaches 280°F (138°C), the soft crack stage (see page 21).

4 As soon as the mixture is ready, remove the pan from the heat and carefully dip the base in cold water to stop the cooking process. Pour the mixture into the prepared cake pan.

5 Allow the syrup to cool for a few minutes until it starts to harden and a knife run across the surface leaves a mark, then score it into squares, cutting almost all the way through.

6 When the mixture has cooled, tip it out of the cake pan and snap it into pieces along the lines you scored. Store the pieces in an airtight container for up to 3 months.

COOK'S NOTES

Keep a close eye on the mixture as it boils and reaches the desired temperature, as it can very quickly go from nearly done to burnt.

Tropical Delights

THESE CHOCOLATEY TREATS ARE MADE FROM CAROB, WHICH CAN BE USED AS A CHOCOLATE
SUBSTITUTE IN MOST RECIPES. IT DOESN'T GIVE SUCH A GLOSSY FINISH, BUT—UNLIKE
CHOCOLATE—IS CAFFEINE-FREE, GLUTEN-FREE, AND CONTAINS NO OXALIC ACID.

You will need

○ ½ cup (175g) clear honey

○ ½ cup (150g) light corn syrup

○ ⅓ cup (75g) unsalted butter, diced

○ ⅔ cup (100g) tropical dried fruit mix,
chopped, plus extra to decorate

○ ½ cup (100g) carob, chopped

Makes 25 squares

1 Grease a shallow 7 inch (18cm) square cake pan.

2 Place a candy thermometer in a bowl of hot
water to warm up, then place the honey, syrup, and
butter in a saucepan and heat, stirring gently, until
the butter has melted.

3 Bring the mixture to the boil, put the candy
thermometer in the saucepan and continue to boil
until the syrup reaches the hard ball stage: 250°F
(121°C) (see page 21).

4 Remove the pan from the heat and carefully
dip the base into cold water to stop the cooking
process. Stir in the tropical dried fruit mix (reserve a
handful for decorating later) then pour the mixture
evenly into the prepared cake pan.

5 Melt the carob in a heat-resistant bowl over a pan
of simmering water, as you would melt chocolate
(see page 31), stirring occasionally to ensure that it
is smooth and free of lumps.

6 Pour the melted carob into the cake pan to cover
the tropical mix and syrup mixture completely.
Scatter the reserved chopped tropical mix over the
surface to decorate.

7 When the mixture starts to set, use a knife to
mark it into squares, then leave to set completely
and snap or cut into pieces once it is hard.

ACTIVELY GOOD

CAROB IS MADE FROM THE HUSKS
OF THE FRUIT OF THE CAROB TREE.
IT IS HIGH IN PROTEIN AND CONTAINS
TANNINS THAT ARE RICH IN GALLIC ACID,
WHICH IS THOUGHT TO HAVE ANTISEPTIC
AND ANTI-BACTERIAL PROPERTIES, AS WELL
AS HELPING TO PREVENT ALLERGIES. THE
TANNINS MAY ALSO HELP TO IMPROVE
DIGESTIVE HEALTH AND INSOLUBLE FIBERS
IN CAROB MAY HELP TO REGULATE BLOOD
SUGAR LEVELS, MAKING THIS A USEFUL
SWEET TREAT FOR DIABETES SUFFERERS.

Nutty Butterscotch Rounds

THE NUTS AND CAROB IN THESE DELICIOUS DISCS ARE PACKED WITH PROTEIN
AND GOODNESS. USE SEMISWEET CHOCOLATE IN PLACE OF THE CAROB, IF YOU PREFER,
BUT THE FINISHED CANDIES WILL BE VERY SWEET.

You will need

○ 1 cup (225g) light brown sugar
○ ¼ cup (60ml) water
○ 1½oz (40g) unsalted butter, diced
○ ½oz (15g) each of shelled, chopped pecan nuts,
pine kernels, and pumpkin seeds
○ 1oz (25g) carob, chopped

Makes 12

1 Oil a baking sheet and put your candy
thermometer in a bowl of hot water to warm.

2 Place the sugar and water in a heavy saucepan
and heat gently, stirring occasionally, until the
sugar has dissolved.

3 Put the candy thermometer in the pan, bring the
mixture to the boil—don't stir at this point—and
then boil until it reaches the soft crack stage: 280°F
(138°C) (see page 21).

4 Remove the pan from the heat and dip the base
of the pan in cold water, then gradually add the
diced butter. Leave it to sit until the mixture is
starting to thicken.

5 Spoon out flat discs of the mixture onto the
prepared baking sheet, then sprinkle each disc with
the nuts and seeds, and leave to set.

6 Once the butterscotch discs have set hard, melt
the carob in a small, heat-resistant bowl set over
a small pan of simmering water as you would
melt chocolate (see page 31), stirring until it is
completely melted and smooth.

7 Remove the bowl from the heat and use a spoon
to drizzle the melted carob over the butterscotch
rounds. Leave the carob to set before serving.

Fruit and Nut Chocolate Lollipops

YOU CAN USE A MOLD TO MAKE PERFECTLY ROUND LOLLIPOPS, BUT THERE IS A
CHARM IN THE ROUGH EDGES AND HOMEMADE FINISH OF THESE FRUITY AND
NUTTY TREATS. CHOOSE YOUR FAVORITE TOPPINGS FOR THE CHOCOLATE, SUCH
AS PISTACHIO NUTS, DRIED SOUR CHERRIES, OR APRICOTS.

You will need

○ 2 cups (350g) semisweet chocolate chips
○ 24 wooden lollipop sticks
○ 2/3 cup (115g) white chocolate chips
○ 1 cup (150g) mixed dried fruit and nuts, chopped

Makes 24

1 Line several baking sheets with parchment paper.

2 Place 1½ cups (260g) of the semisweet chocolate chips in a heat-resistant bowl and set it over a pan of gently simmering water to melt (see page 31). Stir the chocolate until it is just melted, then remove the bowl from the heat and stir in the remaining semisweet chocolate chips. This will help to prevent the chocolate from becoming grainy.

3 Keep stirring until the chocolate is completely melted and smooth.

4 Spoon rounds of melted chocolate onto the prepared baking sheets as neatly as you can. Work on 6 lollipops at a time, so that the chocolate does not begin to set before you are ready.

5 Position a lollipop stick in each chocolate disc, turning the stick over to make sure that it is completely coated, and checking that it is far enough into the chocolate and is neatly in the center of the disc.

6 Once all the lollipops are finished, leave them to set until they are hard.

7 Melt the white chocolate chips in the same way as the semisweet chocolate, then use a spoon to drizzle it over the chocolate discs.

8 Sprinkle the fruit and nut mixture over the white chocolate before it starts to harden, pressing it in slightly if necessary to make sure it will stick.

9 Leave the completed lollipops to set, then carefully lift them off the baking sheets, using a metal spatula if necessary to help you.

ACTIVELY GOOD

FLAVONOIDS IN CHOCOLATE HAVE
ANTIOXIDANT PROPERTIES THAT CAN HELP
TO KEEP YOUR HEART, VEINS, AND ARTERIES
HEALTHY. TOO MUCH CHOCOLATE IS STILL
NEVER GOOD FOR YOU, BUT A LITTLE A
WEEK CAN REAP REAL HEALTH BENEFITS,
INCLUDING REDUCED BLOOD PRESSURE
AND STRESS LEVELS.

Chocolate-stuffed Prunes

THE SWEET AND CHEWY FLESH OF FIBER-RICH PRUNES MAKES THEM THE PERFECT PARTNER FOR A RICH CHOCOLATE FILLING AND COATING. THESE ARE STRICTLY GROWN-UP CANDIES AND TASTE WONDERFUL WITH COFFEE AT THE END OF A MEAL.

You will need

◦ 24 extra-large pitted, dried prunes (pre-soaked or softened)
◦ 1½oz (40g) unsalted butter
◦ 3oz (75g) blanched almonds, chopped and toasted
◦ 1 egg yolk
◦ 1 tablespoon Amaretto liqueur
◦ ½ cup (90g) semisweet chocolate, melted and cooled

CHOCOLATE FOR DIPPING
◦ 1 cup (200g) plain chocolate pieces
◦ ¼ cup (65g) unsalted butter

Makes 24

1 In a food processor, blend together the butter, almonds, egg yolk, and Amaretto until creamy. With the machine still running, slowly pour in the melted chocolate and mix until well blended.

2 Scrape the chocolate mixture into a bowl and refrigerate for about 1 hour, or until it is firm enough to pipe.

3 Line a baking sheet with wax paper, then take one prune at a time and pipe the chocolate mixture inside to fill them. Use the hole left where the stone has been removed. Lay the stuffed fruits on the prepared baking sheet and chill in the refrigerator for 30 minutes.

4 In a saucepan over a low heat, melt the dipping chocolate and butter together, stirring frequently until smooth. Remove from the heat. Leave the chocolate to cool to room temperature, stirring from time to time to keep it smooth and free of lumps.

5 Spear each stuffed fruit with a toothpick and dip it into the melted chocolate mixture. Allow the excess chocolate to drain back into the bowl, then lay the coated fruit back on the baking sheet for the chocolate to set. Use another toothpick to slide the fruit off its stick if necessary.

6 Refrigerate the fruits for at least 1 hour to allow the chocolate to set before serving.

COOK'S NOTES

This recipe contains raw egg yolk, so it is best avoided by pregnant women, children, the elderly, or other people in an at-risk group, as raw eggs can carry a risk of salmonella. If you can find them, use pasteurized eggs to minimize this risk.
You can make this recipe with dried figs, too. They are a good source of potassium, which can help to control blood pressure.

APPLES & PEARS

It's a well-worn adage that an apple a day keeps the doctor at bay, and there is no denying the myriad health benefits of these staple fruits, from boosting your immune system to reducing the risk of heart disease.

It's not just about vitamin C. Apples are high in this disease-fighting antioxidant, but they also contain high levels of pectin, a fiber that helps to prevent cholesterol from building up on the lining of blood vessels and can, as a result, help to reduce the risk of heart disease and atherosclerosis. This protective property is found in the skin of the apple, but it is still found in apple juice as well as the fresh flesh, so jellies, such as the **Sugared Apple Jelly** (page 79) and **Green Apple Paste** (page 85) should still give you the same benefit.

Pears contain many of the same health benefits as apples. **Pear Drops** (page 78) are a delightful, old-fashioned treat, but pears can also be substituted for apples in the **Sugared Apple Jelly**, **Green Apple Paste**, and **Apple Leather** (page 84) recipes, although pears usually have a more delicate flavor, so the candies may have a more subtle taste.

• Asthma studies have shown that apple juice can help to relieve symptoms in young asthma sufferers, so apple candies can be an alternative to, or offered alongside, sipping fresh apple juice when they start to feel an attack. Flavonoids and phenolic acids in the fruit are thought to help to ease inflammation in the airways and can help to allow the child to breathe more easily.

• Apples are also rich in potassium, which helps to control blood pressure and lower the risk of stroke, making them powerful agents in a dietary attack on serious illness.

• **Toffee Apples** (page 81) don't lose any of the natural goodness of the apple, as the apple itself remains untouched. They are a fun way to add a sweet crunch to your fruit occasionally.

• There is some evidence that an antioxidant found in red apples, called quercetin, can help to combat the effects of age-related mental degeneration and that flavonoids within the fruit can have brain-protecting properties.

• Quercetin can also inhibit the action of enzymes that break down complex carbohydrates into simple sugars, meaning that it can help to regulate blood sugar levels. In addition, other constituents found in apples (polyphenols) help to stimulate insulin production and inhibit the absorption of glucose, which may help to balance out the effects of the sugar consumed in the candies themselves.

• Another flavonoid found only in apples— called phloridzin—may help to increase bone density and can be an important element in protecting post-menopausal women from osteoporosis.

Pear Drops

THIS OLD-FASHIONED FAVORITE IS FLAVORED WITH PEAR JUICE AND EXTRACT AND
HAS A MORE DELICATE FLAVOR THAN THE COMMON SHOP-BOUGHT PEAR
AND BANANA VERSION OF THE SWEET. LOOK FOR NATURAL EXTRACTS
IN HEALTH FOOD STORES.

You will need

- 2 cups (380g) sugar
- Scant 1 cup (130g) powdered glucose
- ³/₄ cup (180ml) unsweetened pear juice
- 1 teaspoon cream of tartar
- A few drops of pear extract
- Confectioners' sugar for coating

Makes about 1¼lb (550g)

1 Oil a cake pan approximately 7 inch (18cm) square and put your candy thermometer in a bowl of hot water to warm.

2 Gently heat the sugar, glucose and pear juice in a heavy saucepan, stirring with a wooden spoon, until the sugar has dissolved. If you cannot find pear juice or juice your own pears, you can simply use water instead.

3 Bring to a boil, and boil for 3 minutes.

4 Place the thermometer in the pan and continue to boil until the temperature reaches 310°F (154°C), the hard crack stage (see page 21).

5 Remove the saucepan from the heat, stir in the cream of tartar and pear extract, and pour the syrup into the prepared cake pan.

6 Leave for a short while until the mixture is just cool enough to handle, then very quickly turn it out of the pan onto a work surface and cut into small pieces using lightly oiled scissors. Form the pieces into small balls. If you don't work fast at this stage, the candy will set hard and you will only be able to break it into shards.

7 Once cool, roll the pear drops in the confectioners' sugar to coat them, then wrap each one in cellophane. Store in an airtight container.

COOK'S NOTES

Adding cream of tartar will help to prevent the sugar in the syrup from crystallizing. If you don't have any, you can substitute another anti-crystallizing agent instead (see page 19), such as lemon juice. For 1 teaspoon of cream of tartar use 3 teaspoons of lemon juice.

Sugared Apple Jelly

SUCKING ON ONE OF THESE LITTLE JELLIES WILL SOOTHE A SORE OR TICKLY THROAT.
USE FRUIT JUICE THAT HAS NOT BEEN MADE WITH CONCENTRATE IF YOU CAN,
TO KEEP THE INGREDIENTS AS NATURAL AS POSSIBLE. BETTER STILL, JUICE
SOME FRESH FRUIT YOURSELF.

You will need

- 1oz (25g) powdered gelatin
- $^2/_3$ cup (150ml) cold water
- $^2/_3$ cup (150ml) clear, unsweetened apple juice
- $^1/_3$ cup (75g) sugar
- 4 tablespoons glucose syrup or corn syrup
- $^1/_3$ cup (60g) superfine sugar, for dusting

Makes about 64 pieces

1 Rinse a cake pan 6 inch (15cm) square. Sprinkle
the gelatin over the water and leave it to soften.

2 Gently heat the fruit juice, sugar, and glucose or
corn syrup in a heavy saucepan until the sugar has
dissolved, stirring with a wooden spoon. Then stir
in the softened gelatin and continue to heat gently,
stirring, until the gelatin has dissolved.

3 Pour the mixture into the wet cake pan and leave
to set in a cool place for at least 6 hours. Turn out
the set jelly onto a cold work surface and cut into
squares with a sharp, wet knife. Dip or roll the
finished jellies in superfine sugar to coat them.

COOK'S NOTES

If you juice or purée your own fruits, pass the
liquid through a cheesecloth-lined strainer or
jelly straining bag to remove any fibers and
leave the juice as clear as possible. A cloudy
juice will not look as jewel-like.

Toffee Apples

No Hallowe'en party or bonfire night is complete without a sugary-sweet toffee apple. Once you've mastered the basic sticky coating, use your imagination and add extra coatings, such as nuts, sesame seeds, or dry, unsweetened coconut.

You will need

○ 8 crisp apples
○ 1½ cups (300g) superfine sugar
○ 1½ cups (350ml) water
○ 8 sturdy wooden skewers or lollipop sticks
○ Additional toppings, such as sesame seeds, sugar sprinkles, nuts, or coconut, optional

Makes 8

1 Start by cleaning the apples to remove any waxy coating on the skin that would stop the caramel from sticking. Place the apples in a large bowl and pour over freshly boiled water. Scoop them out with a slotted spoon and wipe with paper towels until they are completely dry. Put your candy thermometer in the bowl of hot apple water to warm, ready for making the syrup.

2 Twist off any stalks on the apples and push a skewer or lollipop stick through the stalk end and far enough into the core to feel firm, while leaving enough of a stick to hold. Set the apples aside.

3 Line a baking sheet with parchment paper.

4 Make a sugar syrup (see page 18), by putting the sugar and water in a large, heavy saucepan over a medium heat. Stir as it warms until all the sugar has dissolved and the syrup is boiling.

5 Stop stirring at this point and put your candy thermometer in the syrup. Continue to boil the syrup until the temperature reaches 310°F (154°C), the hard crack stage (see page 21) for making

toffee. When it is ready, a little of the toffee mixture dripped into a bowl of very cold water should instantly set hard and be brittle when taken out. The toffee must be hard, not chewy.

6 Once the syrup is ready, remove the pan from the heat and carefully dip the base in cold water to stop the cooking process and prevent the syrup from burning. Working quickly, but carefully, dip each apple—one at a time—into the toffee mixture, rolling it round until it is completely covered.

7 Lift out the apple and let the excess toffee drip back into the pan, then roll or dip the apple in any other coating you are using, before transferring the toffee apple to the prepared baking sheet to set.

Actively Good

They may be coated in a sugary toffee, but the apples at the heart of this sweet treat still pack a healthy punch. They are fiber-rich, contain pectin, which can help to reduce cholesterol and the risk of atherosclerosis and heart disease, and are high in potassium, too, which helps to keep blood pressure under control.

Chocolate-covered Apple Slices

WAFER THIN APPLE CRISPS GET A TOUCH OF LUXURY WITH THE HEAT OF
CINNAMON AND A BITTER CHOCOLATE COATING. THEY MAKE A LOVELY,
FRESH ALTERNATIVE TO AFTER DINNER MINTS.

You will need

- 1 large apple, washed and dried
- 1 teaspoon ground cinnamon
- 7oz (200g) semisweet or bittersweet chocolate, broken into pieces

Makes 8–10 slices

1 Turn the oven to its lowest setting. Line a large baking sheet with parchment paper.

2 Using a mandoline or very sharp knife, cut the apple into very thin slices.

3 Arrange the apple slices on the prepared baking sheet in a single layer and sprinkle with the cinnamon. Bake in the oven for 45–60 minutes, or until dried and slightly crisp. Remove from the oven then transfer the paper with the apples on to a wire rack and leave to cool completely.

4 Melt the chocolate in a heat-resistant bowl set over a pan of simmering water (see page 31). Remove from the heat and stir gently until smooth.

5 Using a skewer or dipping fork (see page 15), dip the apple slices into the melted chocolate to cover them completely, then place on clean parchment paper to set.

Apple Leather

CHILDREN WILL LOVE THIS CHEWY, STRETCHY, STICKY CANDY AND IT GIVES A
GREAT INSTANT ENERGY BOOST AS A SNACK. TRY ADDING GROUND CINNAMON TO
THE MIXTURE OR PUTTING A FEW WHOLE CLOVES IN THE WATER WHEN COOKING
THE FRUIT FOR A LITTLE SPICE AND HEAT.

You will need

- 5 apples (enough to yield 4 cups (700g) of peeled, cored, and chopped fruit)
- Approximately 2 cups (450ml) water
- Sugar, to taste
- Lemon juice, to taste
- Ground cinnamon, nutmeg, or cloves, to taste, optional

Makes enough for 1 large baking sheet

1 Peel, core, and chop the apples. Taste a piece to gauge how sweet the fruit is: this will help you to decide how much sugar you will need to add.

2 Put the apple pieces in a large, heavy saucepan with 1/2 cup (120ml) water for each cup of chopped fruit. Bring to a simmer and cook until the fruit is just tender. Remove from the heat.

3 Without draining the cooking water, use a potato masher to mash the fruit. If you have one, you could pass the cooked fruit mixture through a mouli, or press it through a strainer. Alternatively, use an immersion (stick) blender or food processor.

4 Taste the purée and add a little sugar, lemon juice and spice, if using, until you have the flavor you want (see Cook's Notes, opposite).

5 Return the purée to the pan if you took it out to purée it, and bring it back to a simmer for 5–10 minutes, until the purée has thickened. Remove

from the heat. Use the blender, strainer, or mouli again to make sure that the purée is really smooth, and check and adjust the flavoring one last time.

6 Line a baking sheet that has a shallow lip with strong plastic wrap (microwave-safe grade) and pour in the purée. It should be no more than 1/4in (5mm) thick—the thinner, the better.

7 Place the baking sheet in a preheated oven at 250ºF (121ºC) for 15 minutes, then turn off the heat, leave the door closed, and leave the fruit leather to dry out overnight, until the surface is smooth and it is no longer sticky. Peel the leather away from the plastic wrap and roll it up to store.

COOK'S NOTES

Adjust the flavorings little by little. For each
4 cups (700g) of chopped fruit, add sugar
1 tablespoon at a time, or lemon juice
1 teaspoon at a time. If you decide to add
ground cinnamon, nutmeg or other ground
spices, do it a pinch at a time; look for ground
cloves if you can, or add whole cloves to the first
cooking stage and pick them out of the mixture
before puréeing it for the first time.

Green Apple Paste

THESE REFRESHING APPLE SWEETS MAKE A FLAVORFUL, GUILT-FREE TREAT WHEN
YOU NEED SOMETHING SMALL AND SWEET TO EAT. ADD A LITTLE NATURAL
GREEN FOOD COLORING AT STEP 4 FOR A REALLY VIBRANT COLOR, IF YOU LIKE.

You will need

- 2¼lb (1kg) Granny Smith apples
- 4 cups (1¾ pints/1 liter) cold water
- 1¼–1½ cups (250–300g) sugar
- Juice of ½ lemon
- A little natural green food coloring (optional)

Makes 24–36 pieces

1 Roughly chop the apples and place in a large saucepan. Add just enough water to cover the apples, bring to the boil, then simmer for 15 minutes, or until the apples are very soft.

2 Strain the apples, then push them through a strainer into a heatproof bowl. Weigh the purée into a clean saucepan, then add half the total weight of purée in sugar to the pan.

3 Cook, uncovered, over a very low heat, stirring regularly, for about 1½ hours or until the mixture becomes very thick and smooth, and a line drawn through the paste remains.

4 Remove from the heat and stir in the lemon juice then return to the very low heat for 5 minutes or so, stirring.

5 Line a shallow 7½ inch (19cm) square cake pan with parchment paper. Transfer the apple paste to the pan and spread evenly (the mixture should be about ½–5/8in (1–1.5cm) thick. Leave to cool until completely cold and set firmly enough to cut easily.

6 Turn out the paste onto a parchment paper-lined chopping board and peel off the lining paper. Cut the paste into even pieces or squares. Store in an airtight container in the refrigerator or in a cool place, with wax paper between each layer, and eat within a few days (during storage the pieces of apple paste may become slightly sticky).

SUMMER BERRIES

STRAWBERRIES, RASPBERRIES, CRANBERRIES, BLUEBERRIES, AND MORE. THERE ARE
SO MANY DELICIOUS AND COLORFUL SUMMER BERRIES YOU CAN LET YOUR
IMAGINATION INSPIRE YOU AND ADAPT THESE RECIPES TO SUIT WHAT IS
MOST ABUNDANT IN YOUR GARDEN OR FRESHEST IN THE STORES.

You don't need to restrict yourself to making these candies only in summer; many summer fruits can be bought frozen throughout the year and used in just the same way—and in the same quantities—as their fresh, summer equivalents. You don't even need to use fresh fruit: the **Strawberry and Raspberry Creams** (page 88) are made with a jammy, conserve center, which you can make yourself from fresh berries, or spoon from a shop-bought jar. The candies will be just as irresistible either way.

- Strawberries and raspberries are high in vitamin C: a powerful and fast-working antioxidant that will help to combat multiple different ailments and will strengthen your all-round immunity.
- Raspberries contain an extraordinary range of antioxidants and anti-inflammatory phytonutrients that may help to combat a number of chronic diseases, including atherosclerosis, type 2 diabetes, and hypertension. **Raspberry Jujubes** (page 89) and **Mixed Berry Fruit Leather** (page

95) are made by puréeing the whole fruit and this makes them excellent candies for maximizing the benefits of the fruit ingredients.

- For recipes that call for fruit juice as an ingredient, you may choose from a range of juices available in the supermarkets. Most are interchangable in these recipes, such as **Summer Fruit Jellies** (page 92) and **Summer Fruit Lollipops** (page 90). Better still, juice your own fresh fruits, so that you know the fruit has been processed as little as possible and is not produced from a concentrate. Pass the juice through a cheesecloth-lined strainer or a jelly strainer to remove any traces of flesh and make sure that it is as clear as possible to make the candies as jewel-like and clear as possible, too.
- The blueberries in **White Chocolate and Blueberry Fudge** (page 94) are widely hailed as a superfood, as they have one of the highest antioxidant levels of all fruits and vegetables. Blueberries are thought to protect against urinary tract infections, cancer, brain degeneration, and cardiovascular diseases. To reap their greatest benefits they are best eaten fresh and raw, but the dried fruits in this recipe will still offer some of the positive health effects of the berries.

Strawberry and Raspberry Creams

IF YOU MAKE YOUR OWN PRESERVES, HOMEMADE JAM IS DELICIOUS IN THESE
FONDANT CREAMS; IF NOT, BUY A GOOD QUALITY JAM THAT IS NOT TOO
CHUNKY—YOU JUST NEED A DROP IN THE CENTER OF EACH CHOCOLATE.

You will need

6oz (175g) fondant made from:

○ 1 cup (190g) sugar

○ 1/3 cup (75ml) water

○ 1/2 tablespoon glucose syrup or corn syrup

○ Confectioners' sugar, for dusting

○ 1 1/3 cups (230g) semisweet chocolate pieces

○ 1/2 cup (170g) preserve: strawberry and raspberry mixed, or some of each

Makes 24

1 Make the fondant the day before (see page 24) and leave it to rest overnight.

2 Melt the chocolate in a heat-resistant bowl set over a pan of simmering water (see page 31), then spoon a little at a time into the sections of a fondant mold, or into individual foil candy cases. Carefully tip the molds until the sides and bases are all evenly coated and then pour any excess chocolate back into the bowl. Leave the chocolate cases to set in a cool place for around 30 minutes.

3 Put the fondant in a saucepan and heat it gently —just enough to soften it—then spoon a little into each chocolate case until it is almost full. Leave the fondant to set.

4 When the fondant is firm, use a skewer or small knife to make a small hole in each one and add a little strawberry or raspberry preserve. Smooth the fondant back over to cover the hole.

5 Gently reheat the chocolate to make sure that it is melted and smooth, then carefully add a little to each mold to cover the fondant, and leave the chocolates in a cool place to set hard.

COOK'S NOTES

You can use other flavors of preserve for this recipe, if you prefer. Try a mixed berry, blueberry, or cherry preserve instead to vary the flavors of the candies. These candies make a lovely gift, wrapped in cellophane and tied with a colorful ribbon or string.

Raspberry Jujubes

THESE RASPBERRY CANDIES HAVE AN INTENSE BERRY FLAVOR AND A BRILLIANT JEWEL-LIKE COLOR. TRY MAKING THEM WITH ANY SUMMER BERRIES OR CURRANTS YOU HAVE, OR EVEN A MIXTURE. YOU MAY NEED TO ADD MORE SUGAR IF THE FRUIT IS TART.

You will need

- 1oz (25g) powdered gelatin
- ²/₃ cup (150ml) cold water
- ½ cup (95g) sugar
- 1¼ cups (600ml) raspberry purée, strained, made from 4 cups (550g) fruit
- Superfine sugar, for coating, optional

Makes about ½ lb (225g)

1 Rinse a cake pan approximately 6 inch (15cm) square to wet it inside. Sprinkle the gelatin over the cold water and leave it to soften.

2 Mix the gelatin mixture and sugar together in a large, heavy-based saucepan, then stir in the raspberry purée.

3 Heat gently, stirring with a wooden spoon, until the sugar and gelatin have dissolved, then bring to a boil, and boil for 5 minutes.

4 Remove from the heat, pour the mixture into the prepared cake pan and leave it to set overnight. The next day, dip the base of the cake pan briefly in hot water to release the candy, then tip it out onto a work surface.

5 Use a wet, sharp knife or wet cookie cutters to cut the candies into squares, diamonds, or fancy shapes. Roll or dip the finished candies in superfine sugar to coat them, if you wish.

Summer Fruit Lollipops

YOU CAN CUSTOMIZE THIS BASIC LOLLIPOP RECIPE BY ADDING PIECES OF CHOPPED
FRUIT, SUGAR STRANDS OR BALLS, OR EVEN EDIBLE GLITTER. OR USE ANY FRUIT
JUICE YOU LIKE, SUCH AS LEMON AND LIME WITH A LITTLE GRATED RIND.
USE YOUR IMAGINATION OR LET YOUR CHILDREN HELP.

You will need

○ ½ cup (120ml) summer berries fruit juice
○ 1 cup (190g) sugar
○ ¼ cup (60ml) water
○ A few drops of natural red food coloring, optional
○ 15 lollipop sticks

Makes 15 lollipops

1 Put a candy thermometer in hot water to warm
and line 2 baking sheets with parchment paper.

2 Put the fruit juice in a small, heavy saucepan
and boil to reduce it to a syrup until you only have
about 2 tablespoons left in the pan. Set aside.

3 Make a sugar syrup (see page 18) with the sugar
and water, add the thermometer to the saucepan
and boil until the temperature reaches 300°F
(149°C), the hard crack stage. Remove from the
heat, carefully dip the base of the pan in cold
water to stop the cooking process, then mix in the
reserved fruit juice syrup, and the coloring if you
want to boost the brightness of the lollipops.

4 Carefully spoon blobs of the syrup onto the
baking sheets, 5 at a time, leaving room between
them so that the lollipops don't merge together. Put
a lollipop stick in each puddle of syrup, turn the
stick over so that it is covered on both sides and
make sure that it is surrounded by syrup.

5 Continue until you have used all the mixture; if it
starts to get too thick to spoon out, return the pan to
the heat briefly until the mixture loosens up again.
Leave the lollipops to set for 30 minutes.

White Chocolate and Strawberry Bars

These sumptuous, melt-in-the-mouth, strawberry-flavored white chocolate bars are ideal for an after-dinner sweet treat. Dry some extra strawberries at the same time and use them as a snack or to top a bowl of ice cream.

You will need

- 5 strawberries, hulled, rinsed, dried, and halved
- 12oz (350g) white chocolate for cooking, broken into squares or roughly chopped
- 1 scant cup (100g) chopped strawberries
- A few whole (shelled) pistachio nuts, to decorate

Makes 2 large bars, or 32 pieces

1 Dry the halved strawberries in the oven before preparing the rest of the recipe. Preheat the oven to 225°F (110°C) and line a baking sheet with wax paper. Lay the strawberries, cut-side-up, on the baking sheet and place in the oven for 3–4 hours.

2 Lightly oil and line two 2lb (900g) loaf pans with parchment paper. Melt the white chocolate over a pan of simmering water (see page 31).

3 Mash the chopped strawberries then press through a fine strainer to make a smooth purée. Put the purée in a small saucepan, and heat gently.

4 Put 5–6 tablespoons of the purée in a bowl over the pan of simmering water you used for the chocolate. Gradually add the melted chocolate, stirring until smooth and combined.

5 Pour the strawberry chocolate into the loaf pans, then spread it in an even layer. Arrange the dried strawberries and pistachios on top, then set aside to cool completely. Once cool, place in the refrigerator (uncovered) until firm enough to cut.

6 Once set, turn out the chocolate onto a cutting board and peel off the lining paper, then turn over the bars and cut into pieces using a sharp knife.

Summer Fruit Jellies

ADAPT THIS RECIPE TO USE ANY FLAVORED FRUIT JUICE YOU LIKE. IF YOU JUICE YOUR
OWN FRUIT, PASS IT THROUGH A JELLY STRAINING BAG OR CHEESECLOTH-LINED
STRAINER TO REMOVE ANY FIBERS THAT WILL MAKE THE FINISHED JELLIES CLOUDY.

You will need

- 1oz (25g) powdered gelatin
- 4 tablespoons cold water
- $^2/_3$ cup (140ml) clear, unsweetened fruit juice (raspberry, strawberry, or blackcurrant), strained if necessary
- $^1/_3$ cup (70g) sugar
- 4 tablespoons glucose syrup or corn syrup
- Superfine sugar, for coating, optional

Makes about 1lb (450g)

1 Rinse a cake pan approximately 6 inch (15cm) square to wet it.

2 Sprinkle the gelatin over the water in a small bowl and leave it to soften.

3 Gently heat the fruit juice, sugar and glucose or corn syrup in a heavy saucepan until the sugar has dissolved, stirring with a wooden spoon.

4 Stir in the softened gelatin and continue to heat gently, stirring, until the gelatin has dissolved.

5 Remove from the heat, pour the mixture into the prepared cake pan and leave the jelly to set in a cool place for at least 6 hours.

6 Turn the jelly out of the cake pan onto a cold work surface and cut into squares or shapes with a wet, sharp knife or cookie cutter.

7 Serve plain or roll in superfine sugar to coat all over, if you like.

8 Plain or sugar-coated jellies can be kept in an airtight container in a cool place for a few days.

COOK'S NOTES

Homemade jellies may not have the vibrant, jewel-like coloring of their store-bought equivalents. If you want to boost the color of your sweets, you could add a few drops of natural food coloring to the fruit juice mixture. Always look for natural, non-synthetic colorings, sold in good grocers and health food stores.

White Chocolate and Blueberry Fudge

THE WHITE CHOCOLATE GIVES THIS FUDGE A LUXURIOUS, SILKY TEXTURE AND THE SLIGHTLY SHARP FLAVOR OF THE BLUEBERRIES HELPS TO STOP THE SWEETNESS FROM BEING CLOYING. TRY USING OTHER DRIED FRUITS, LIKE CRANBERRIES OR CHERRIES, TOO.

You will need

- 1 cup (200g) sugar
- 1½ tablespoons (20g) butter
- ¼ teaspoon salt
- ½ cup (120ml) sweetened condensed milk
- 1 teaspoon vanilla extract
- 1⅓ cups (250g) white chocolate, chopped
- ¾ cup (125g) dried blueberries

Makes about 1lb (450g)

1 Grease a 9 inch (23cm) square baking pan.

2 Put the sugar, butter, salt, condensed milk, and vanilla in a heavy saucepan over a medium heat and bring the mixture to the boil. Stir the mixture as it heats up to prevent it catching and burning on the bottom of the pan.

3 Reduce the heat as soon as the mixture starts to boil, and simmer for 5 minutes, stirring all the time.

4 Remove the pan from the heat and stir in the chocolate pieces; give them a few minutes to start to melt in the hot mixture, then stir until the chocolate has melted completely and is thoroughly incorporated. Next, stir in the blueberries.

5 Pour the mixture into the prepared baking pan, spreading evenly, and leave it to cool to room temperature, then put it in the refrigerator overnight to set completely.

6 Cut the finished fudge into pieces and store in an airtight container in a cool place for up to 3 weeks.

ACTIVELY GOOD

BLUEBERRIES CONTAIN COMPOUNDS THAT CAN HELP TO PREVENT URINARY TRACT INFECTIONS BY STOPPING BACTERIA FROM CONGREGATING ON YOUR BLADDER WALL. SOME STUDIES CLAIM THAT THE ANTHOCYANINS THAT GIVE THE BERRIES THEIR BLUE COLOR ARE ANTIOXIDANTS THAT CAN ALSO DESTROY CANCER-CAUSING FREE RADICALS. THERE IS OTHER EVIDENCE TO SUGGEST THAT FLAVONOIDS IN THE BERRIES WORK AS BRAIN BOOSTERS AND CAN SLOW DOWN OR EVEN HELP TO REVERSE AGE-RELATED MEMORY LOSS.

Mixed Berry Fruit Leather

USE ANY COMBINATION OF SUMMER OR AUTUMN BERRIES YOU LIKE IN THIS RECIPE.
IT'S A GREAT WAY TO USE UP A GLUT OF HOMEGROWN OR FORAGED FRUITS,
ESPECIALLY ONES THAT ARE TOO RIPE TO EAT FRESH.

You will need

- 2 cups (200g) mixed, fresh berries, such as blackberries and raspberries
- ½ cup (120ml) water
- Sugar, to taste

Makes enough for 1 large baking sheet

1 Wash and pick over the berries to remove any stalks or leaves, then put them in a large, heavy saucepan with the water. Bring to a simmer and cook until the fruit is just tender.

2 Remove from the heat, and without draining the cooking water, purée the fruit using an immersion blender or by passing it through a strainer or mouli. Add a little more water if the purée is very thick.

3 Taste the purée and add a little sugar if it tastes too sharp, then return it to the pan and simmer for 5–10 minutes, until the purée has thickened. Remove from the heat and use the immersion blender, strainer or mouli again to make sure that the purée is really smooth.

4 Line a baking sheet that has a shallow lip with strong plastic wrap (microwave safe grade) and pour in the purée. It should be no more than ¼in (5mm) thick, but the thinner, the better.

5 Place the baking sheet in a preheated oven at 250°F (121°C) for 15 minutes. Don't open the door, but turn off the oven and leave the leather to dry out in the oven overnight, until the surface is smooth and it is no longer sticky. Peel the leather away from the plastic wrap and roll it up to store.

COOK'S NOTES

You can make this recipe with frozen berries, too. Heat them in the pan without adding any water to thaw and soften, stirring often. Add a little water (up to ¼ cup/60ml) as you blend the fruit to a purée, if the mixture is very thick.

Herbs & Flowers

MINT

MANY OLD–TIME FAVORITE CANDIES, LIKE PEPPERMINT CREAMS, START WITH THE
FRESH TASTE OF MINT. BUT THEY'RE NOT JUST SWEET AND STICKY—THE LEAVES AND
ESSENTIAL OILS OF PEPPERMINT HAVE GREAT HEALING PROPERTIES, TOO.

Peppermint is a tried and tested remedy for indigestion and that particular, doubled-up tummy ache you get when you've overindulged in far too much rich food. The mint stimulates the production of saliva, which—in turn—boosts the production of digestive enzymes to help the body to digest a heavy meal and relieve the discomfort that comes with it. Most of the candy recipes in the pages that follow use a peppermint extract or oil, rather than the fresh leaves. Avoid synthetic peppermint flavorings and look for extract made from the leaves themselves, and if you are using peppermint oil, always make sure that it is food-grade peppermint oil, and not an essential oil intended for aromatherapy.

- The leaves contain constituents that help to calm the gut, and can relieve wind, colic and the symptoms of irritable bowel syndrome. These active constituents are still found in peppermint oil, and they work by relaxing the muscles that surround the intestine to prevent spasms of stomach pain and indigestion. Keep a supply of **Clear Mints** (page 104) on hand if you are prone to suffering like this.

- Mint is also helpful for calming frayed nerves and soothing headaches—and when you are suffering, there's no more delicious way to take your treatment than by combining it with chocolate, such as in **White Chocolate Peppermint Bark** (page 102) or the classic favorite, **Chocolate Peppermint Creams** (page 101).

- Sucking any boiled sweet will help to soothe a sore throat by stimulating saliva production that will then lubricate the throat, but by choosing a mint candy, like the **Pulled Mint Candies** (page 100), the menthol vapors will help to clear nasal, sinus and chest congestion at the same time. Try **Mint Lollipops** (page 104) as the perfect treat for a poorly child—or to make them a bit more grown-up, lay a small, washed mint leaf on each disc of syrup as you make the lollipops, then cover the leaves with a little more syrup to encase them in the finished candy.

- Peppermint oil also contains anti-microbial properties, which can help to prevent the growth of bacteria and may help to fight infections within the body.

Pulled Mint Candies

FOLLOW THE TECHNIQUES SHOWN ON PAGES 28–30 TO MAKE THESE DUAL-COLORED
PULLED CANDIES. YOU COULD ADD NATURAL FOOD COLORING TO THE SYRUP IF YOU
PREFER, OR JUST PULL ONE HALF TO AN OPAQUE FINISH AND LEAVE THE OTHER CLEAR.

You will need

- 2 cups (380g) sugar
- 1 tablespoon glucose syrup or corn syrup
- ⅔ cup (150ml) water
- ¼ teaspoon cream of tartar
- Peppermint extract

Makes about 1lb (450g)

1 Oil a marble slab or baking sheet and put a candy thermometer in a bowl of hot water to warm.

2 Gently heat the sugar, glucose or corn syrup, and water in a heavy saucepan, stirring with a wooden spoon, until the sugar has dissolved.

3 Add the cream of tartar, bring to a boil, and boil for 3 minutes.

4 Put the candy thermometer in the syrup and continue to boil until the temperature reaches 290°F (143°C), the soft crack stage. Remove the pan from the heat and dip the base in cold water to stop the cooking process. Mix in a few drops of peppermint extract to flavor the syrup.

5 Pour the syrup into 2 pools on the oiled surface.

6 As the syrup cools, lift the edges of each pool with an oiled metal scraper or metal spatula and fold them into the center.

7 With oiled hands, form 1 pool into a roll, then pull and twist the roll until it becomes opaque, much paler in color and has a satin finish. Fold over twice lengthways to form 4 strands, then twist these together, pulling gently, to make a long rope.

8 Form the second pool of syrup into a roll, then pull it into a rope the same length as the first piece.

9 Lay the two pieces side by side, twist them together, then fold the length that is formed over and over to make a short rope.

10 Gently, but firmly and quickly, and giving a twist as you work, pull along the length of the rope one last time.

11 Using lightly oiled, strong scissors, cut the rope into small pieces, giving the rope a half turn towards you with each cut so that the pieces have a traditional triangular surface.

12 Store the candies between layers of wax paper in an airtight container.

COOK'S NOTES

These candies, individually wrapped in celloophane, make lovely gifts, when bundled into an attractive candy box or wicker basket.

Chocolate Peppermint Creams

THESE MINTY CHOCOLATE DISCS WILL MELT IN YOUR MOUTH. THIS RECIPE USES UNCOOKED
FONDANT, BUT YOU COULD ALSO USE A BATCH OF BOILED FONDANT (PAGES 24–25).
DECORATE THE FINISHED CANDIES WITH A DRIZZLE OF WATER ICING OR SUGAR BALLS.

You will need

○ 2 cups (265g) confectioners' sugar, plus
extra for dusting

○ 1 egg white

○ A few drops of peppermint oil

○ ⅔ cup (100g) semisweet or bittersweet
chocolate pieces

Makes about ½lb (225g)

1 Lightly dust the work surface, a rolling pin and a
small round cookie cutter with confectioners' sugar.

2 Whisk the egg white in a bowl until it is foamy,
then add 4 drops of peppermint oil and enough
confectioners' sugar to make a stiff, but pliable
paste. Don't add all the sugar at once, but little by
little until the consistency is right.

3 Turn the fondant out onto the work surface and
knead it until it is smooth and is not cracking.

4 Roll out the fondant to about ¼in (5mm) thick
and cut into discs with the cookie cutter.

5 Melt the chocolate in a bowl set over a pan of
simmering water (see page 31), stirring it to make
sure that it is smooth and completely melted, then
remove the bowl from the heat.

6 Spear the fondant rounds with a skewer or
dipping fork, one at a time, and dip into the
chocolate to cover them completely. Allow any
excess chocolate to drip back into the bowl, then
set the chocolates on a wire rack to cool and set.

7 If the chocolate in the bowl starts to get stiff,
return it to the heat for a while to melt again.

COOK'S NOTES

If you would prefer to use boiled fondant,
so that the recipe does not contain raw egg,
add the peppermint oil to the syrup before you
start mixing it (see page 24). You can add a
few drops to a plain fondant and mix it in as
you knead the mixture, but it will not be so
easy to incorporate evenly.

White Chocolate Peppermint Bark

YOU CAN USE ANY HOMEMADE, HARD PEPPERMINT CANDIES FOR THIS RECIPE, SUCH AS PULLED MINT CANDIES (PAGE 100) OR CLEAR MINTS (PAGE 104). ALTERNATIVELY, CRUSH LEFTOVER CHRISTMAS CANDY CANES OR OTHER UNWANTED MINT SWEETS.

You will need

○ 2lb (900g) white chocolate, chopped
○ Enough candy canes or peppermints to give 1 cup when crushed into small pieces
○ Few drops of peppermint essence, optional

Makes about 2lb (900g)

1 Line a large baking sheet with parchment paper. Melt the chocolate in a heat-resistant bowl set over a pan of simmering water (see page 31).

2 While the chocolate melts, crush the candy. Put the sweets in a polythene food bag and bash with a rolling pin or hammer until there are no chunks larger than about ¼ inch (5mm).

3 Mix together the crushed candy and melted chocolate, reserving some of the larger chunks of candy to sprinkle over the top. Add a few drops of peppermint essence if you like, for a mintier taste.

4 Pour the mixture onto the prepared baking sheet, spread it evenly in a fairly thin layer, and scatter the leftover candy chunks over the surface.

5 Place in the refrigerator to cool for about 1 hour, then break up the bark into chunks to eat.

COOK'S NOTES

You can use any chocolate for this recipe: white, milk, or semisweet. Try swirling together semisweet and white chocolate as you pour the melted mixture onto the baking sheet to create an attractive marbled bark.

Mint Lollipops

ADD SOME PEPPERMINT OIL TO A BASIC BOILED SWEET RECIPE TO MAKE THESE
PRETTY LOLLIPOPS. SMALL, ROUND LOLLIPOP STICKS OR CAKE POP STICKS ARE
BEST FOR THIS RECIPE—FLAT WOODEN STICKS WILL BE TOO CHUNKY.

You will need

- 2 cups (380g) sugar
- 1 tablespoon powdered glucose
- ⅔ cup (140ml) water
- A few drops of peppermint oil
- 30 lollipop sticks

Makes 30 lollipops

1 Oil a heat-resistant work surface and put a candy thermometer in hot water to warm. Gently heat the sugar, glucose, and water in a heavy saucepan, stirring, until the sugar has dissolved.

2 Bring to a boil and boil for 3 minutes. Then add the candy thermometer and continue to boil until the temperature reaches 265°F (129°C), the hard ball stage (see page 21).

3 Remove the pan from the heat and carefully dip the base into cold water to stop the cooking process. Add a few drops of peppermint oil.

4 Spoon small, round pools of syrup onto the oiled surface and lay a lollipop stick in each pool. Add a little more syrup, if necessary, to cover the sticks.

5 Leave the lollipops to harden, then carefully lift them from the surface and wrap in cellophane.

Clear Mints

KEEP SOME OF THESE SIMPLE MINTS IN A JAR AND YOU'LL ALWAYS HAVE A QUICK
AND EASY REMEDY FOR A TICKLY THROAT OR UNCOMFORTABLE, BLOATED STOMACH.

You will need

- 2 cups (380g) sugar
- ¾ cup (180ml) water
- Scant 1 cup (130g) powdered glucose
- ½ teaspoon peppermint extract

Makes about 1¼lb (550g)

1 Lightly oil a shallow cake pan about 11 x 7 inch (28 x 18cm) and warm a candy thermometer.

2 Gently heat the sugar with the water in a heavy saucepan, stirring with a wooden spoon until the sugar has dissolved. Stir in the glucose, increase the heat, and bring to a boil. Boil for 3 minutes

3 Add the candy thermometer and continue to boil until the temperature reaches 290°F (143°C), the soft crack stage (see page 21).

4 Remove the saucepan from the heat, stir in the peppermint extract and pour the syrup into the cake pan. Cool until it is only just firm enough to handle.

5 Using a metal spatula, turn the mixture out of the pan then, with oiled kitchen scissors and working quickly, cut the mint into squares before it hardens.

Mint Fondant Sticks

THESE CHEWY LOLLIPOPS MAKE A CHANGE FROM HARD CANDY AND HAVE AN
INVIGORATING MINTY TASTE. USE ALL THE MIXTURE TO MAKE THE LOLLIPOPS AND
OMIT THE GREEN STRIPS IF YOU WOULD PREFER TO AVOID USING COLORING.

You will need

- 2 cups (380g) sugar
- 1½ cups (450g) glucose syrup or corn syrup
- 1 cup (225ml) water
- ½ teaspoon peppermint extract
- Natural green food coloring
- 6 lollipop sticks

Makes 6 lollipops

1 Preheat the oven to 325°F (160°C), grease 2 large baking sheets, and warm a candy thermometer in a bowl of hot water.

2 Place the sugar, glucose or corn syrup, and water in a large, oven-proof saucepan. Bring the mixture to a boil, stirring until the sugar has dissolved.

3 Add the candy thermometer to the pan and continue to boil, without stirring, until the mixture reaches 260°F (127°C), the hard ball stage (page 21).

4 Remove the pan from the heat and stir in the peppermint extract. Pour about two-thirds of the mixture onto a baking sheet and leave it to stand until it forms a skin and is cool enough to handle.

5 Add a few drops of green food coloring to the remaining mixture and mix until you have a good minty green. Place it in the oven to stay warm.

6 Spread the uncolored mixture on the baking tray, pulling, pushing and folding with oiled hands, until it is opaque and shiny. Cut into 6 pieces with oiled scissors and mould around the lollipop sticks.

7 Remove the green mixture from the oven and, as soon as the mixture is cool enough to handle,

repeat the kneading as above. Cut the green mixture into strips with oiled scissors and press into or wrap around the lollipops to decorate. Allow the lollipops to cool completely before wrapping in wax paper.

GINGER, HERBS, & SPICES

AROMATIC GINGER ADDS A HEAT AND INTERESTING FLAVOR TO CANDIES THAT WILL CUT THROUGH THE SWEETNESS OF THE OTHER INGREDIENTS. CHOOSE OTHER HERBS AND SPICES, SUCH AS CINNAMON OR NUTMEG, TO GIVE DEPTH TO THE FLAVOR OF YOUR CANDIES AND DIFFERENT HEALING PROPERTIES, TOO.

Ginger has myriad health benefits, from relieving wind to reducing inflammation.

- Try a square or two of **Ginger and Honey Fudge** (page 112) to give you a sweet pick-me-up and offset feelings of nausea—it's a useful stand-by on journeys or if you are pregnant. In fact, ginger can help to ease all the symptoms of travel sickness—nausea, dizziness, and cold sweats—so make a batch of this fudge or some **Herbal Healers** (page 110) made from ginger tea to take with you on a long journey.

- If you have a cold or the symptoms of flu, the combination of ginger and honey can help with that, too, by encouraging your body to sweat out its toxins.

- Gingerols are strong anti-inflammatory compounds found in ginger, which may help to ease the joint pain and swelling of sufferers of osteoarthritis and rheumatoid arthritis.

- Essential oils from cinnamon bark contain active components that can help to inhibit the growth of bacteria and fungi, including the yeast Candida, which causes thrush. Try **Carob Truffles with Honey and Cinnamon** (page 110) if you are susceptible to this common problem.

- Cinnamon can also help to regulate blood sugar levels and reduce spikes in levels after eating, and just the smell of the spice is thought to boost mental sharpness.

- **Herbal Healers** (page 110) can be made with any kind of herbal tea. Choose your favorite flavor or one with healing properties that will help a particular ailment you have.

- Chamomile tea is calming and can help if you suffer from insomnia, as it has sedative properties; sucking on a chamomile flavored Herbal Healer may also help to relieve the symptoms of a cough.

- Lemon balm tea will lift your spirits and may help to improve concentration.

- Rooibos tea is high in vitamin C and has excellent antioxidant properties, which can help to prevent disease and may help to combat some of the effects of aging.

- Nutmeg in the **Nutmeg and Cinnamon Truffles** (page 113) has a wide and often unappreciated range of health benefits. It can help to overcome tiredness and depression and sharpen your brain to help you to concentrate. It also has sedative properties, which can help to soothe aches and pains—the quickest way to benefit from this is by rubbing nutmeg oil where the pain is, but a deliciously chocolatey truffle is certain to help to bring relief.

Barley Sugar Twists

THESE OLD-FASHIONED CANDIES ARE A PERENNIAL TREAT. MANY OF THE HEALTH
BENEFITS OF BARLEY ARE CONTAINED IN THE BARLEY WATER THAT MAKES THESE
BARLEY SUGAR TWISTS, FROM TREATING COUGHS TO RELIEVING GALL STONES.

You will need

- 2 tablespoons pearl barley
- At least 5 cups (1.2 liters) cold water
- Thinly pared rind and juice of ½ lemon
- 2 cups (380g) sugar
- ¼ teaspoon cream of tartar
- 1 teaspoon ground allspice or ground ginger

Makes about 1lb (450g)

1 Put the barley into a saucepan. Stir in 1¼ cups (280ml) water and bring to a boil.

2 Remove from the heat, drain the barley, and rinse it under cold running water.

3 Return the barley to the rinsed saucepan, stir in 3¾ cups (850ml) cold water and the lemon rind. Bring to a boil, reduce the heat, cover and simmer for about 1½–1¾ hours, until the barley is soft.

4 Strain off and reserve the liquid, add the lemon juice and make up to 2½ cups (560ml) with cold water. Discard the barley and the lemon rind.

5 Lightly oil a marble surface or baking sheet and put a candy thermometer in a bowl of hot water to warm up for later.

6 Gently heat the sugar, cream of tartar, allspice or ginger and barley water in a heavy saucepan, stirring constantly with a wooden spoon, until the sugar has dissolved.

7 Bring to a boil, and boil for 3 minutes, then put the candy thermometer in the mixture, and boil until the temperature of the syrup reaches 310°F (154°C), the hard crack stage (see page 21).

8 Pour the syrup onto the oiled surface or baking sheet so that it spreads out to an even pool.

9 Leave the barley sugar to cool until it firms around the edges.

10 Using a lightly oiled metal spatula, ease one edge of the sheet of syrup away from the surface or baking sheet, then pull the edge up with your hands and fold it over the middle of the sheet of syrup, laying it down evenly so there are no wrinkles.

11 Immediately fold the opposite edge over to meet the first edge in the middle.

12 Gently lift the folded sheet using the oiled metal spatula and, cutting alternately from opposite sides of the sheet, cut it into strips about ½ inch (1cm) wide with oiled scissors. Twist each strip into a spiral as it is cut.

13 Leave the twists to cool completely and harden, then wrap them individually in cellophane. Store in an airtight container.

ACTIVELY GOOD

BARLEY'S WATER-SOLUBLE FIBER CAN
HELP TO DISSOLVE AND PREVENT GALL
STONES, AND BARLEY WATER IS ALSO
RECOMMENDED FOR PREVENTING URINARY
TRACT INFECTIONS, PARTICULARLY DURING
PREGNANCY. THE NIACIN (VITAMIN B)
IN BARLEY CAN ALSO HELP TO REDUCE
CHOLESTEROL, AND BARLEY WATER
IS A NATURAL DIURETIC, TO EASE
WATER RETENTION.

Herbal Healers

USING HERBAL TEA BAGS IS AN EASY WAY TO INCORPORATE THE HEALTH BENEFITS
OF A WIDE RANGE OF HERBS INTO YOUR CANDIES. CHOOSE YOUR FAVORITE VARIETY,
OR CHOOSE ONE TO COMBAT A PARTICULAR AILMENT OR PROBLEM.

You will need

- 4 herbal teabags
- 2 cups (480ml) boiling water
- 2 cups (380g) sugar
- Confectioners' sugar, for dusting

Makes about 1lb (450g)

1 Brew the tea bags in the boiling water for 20 minutes, line a baking pan with parchment paper, and put a candy thermometer in hot water to warm.

2 Put the sugar in a heavy saucepan and strain the tea into the pan. Heat slowly, stirring until the sugar has dissolved completely, then bring to a boil.

3 Put the thermometer in the pan and continue to boil, without stirring, until the mixture reaches 300°F (149°C), the hard crack stage (see page 21). Remove the pan from the heat and carefully dip the base into cold water to stop the cooking process.

4 Pour the mixture into the prepared pan, allow it to cool slightly, then cut into strips, then small pieces, while still warm. Leave to harden, then toss in confectioners' sugar to finish.

OPPOSITE: HERBAL HEALERS

Carob Truffles with Honey and Cinnamon

HONEY AND CINNAMON ARE A TIMELESS COMBINATION FOR COMBATING THE
SYMPTOMS OF COUGHS AND SORE THROATS. THESE CHOCOLATEY, BITE-SIZE TRUFFLES
ARE ACTUALLY MADE WITH CAROB, A CAFFEINE-FREE ALTERNATIVE TO CHOCOLATE.

You will need

- 3 tablespoons unsweetened carob powder
- 1 tablespoon instant coffee powder
- 2 tablespoons clear honey
- 1 tablespoon unsalted butter, diced
- ¼ cup (30g) instant, nonfat dry milk
- Unsweetened carob powder flavored with ground cinnamon, for coating

Makes about 10

1 Mix the carob and coffee powders in a heat-resistant bowl. Add the honey, place the bowl over a saucepan of simmering water and heat, stirring, until the ingredients are evenly blended.

2 Remove from the heat and mix in the butter and dry milk until melted and combined.

3 Cool a little, then form the mixture into small balls. Roll each one lightly in carob powder flavored with ground cinnamon.

4 Place in small paper candy cases. Cover and leave in a cool place overnight before eating.

Ginger and Honey Fudge

SOOTHE A SORE THROAT WITH THESE MELT-IN-THE-MOUTH SQUARES OF FUDGE.
GINGER CAN HELP TO ENCOURAGE YOUR BODY TO 'SWEAT OUT' COLDS AND FLU, SO
THIS SWEET TREAT CAN DO MORE THAN JUST MAKE YOU FEEL BETTER.

You will need

- 1½ cups (300g) sugar
- ¼ cup (60ml/85g) clear honey
- ¼ cup (60g) unsalted butter, diced
- ⅔ cup (140ml) milk
- A few drops of ginger extract
- ¾ cup (180g) preserved ginger, well drained and finely chopped

Makes about 1¼lb (550g)

1 Butter or oil a cake pan approximately 7 x 5 inch (18 x 13cm) and put a candy thermometer in a bowl of hot water to warm.

2 Gently heat the sugar, honey, butter, and milk in a heavy saucepan, stirring with a wooden spoon, until the sugar has dissolved and the honey melted.

3 Bring to a boil, and boil for 3 minutes.

4 Put the candy thermometer in the pan, and continue to boil until the temperature reaches 240°F (116°C), the soft ball stage (see page 21).

5 Dip the base of the saucepan in cold water to stop the mixture from cooking any more, then add the ginger extract and chopped ginger and beat until the mixture becomes thick and paler in color.

6 Pour into the prepared cake pan and cool until it is just beginning to set. Then mark the fudge into squares with a lightly oiled, sharp knife and leave to cool and set completely.

7 Cut or break the finished fudge into pieces. Store between layers of wax paper in a cool place, in an airtight container.

Nutmeg and Cinnamon Truffles

THE WARM AND WOODY FLAVORS OF NUTMEG AND CINNAMON GIVE THESE CHOCOLATEY TRUFFLES A TASTE OF WINTER. NUTMEG CAN HELP TO BEAT TIREDNESS AND IMPROVE CONCENTRATION, SO THEY MAKE A GREAT PICK-ME-UP WHEN YOU ARE WEARY.

You will need

- ¾ cup (175ml) heavy cream
- 1 teaspoon ground cinnamon
- ¼–½ teaspoon ground or freshly grated nutmeg
- 5oz (150g) semisweet or bittersweet chocolate, chopped
- 2½oz (75g) milk chocolate, chopped
- ½ cup (75g) chopped roasted hazelnuts
- Unsweetened cocoa powder, for dusting

Makes 20–25 truffles

1 Put the cream and ground spices in a saucepan and bring to a boil. Remove from the heat and pour over both the chopped chocolates in a bowl.

2 Stir gently until smooth, then add the hazelnuts and stir to combine. Leave to cool. Cover and chill in the refrigerator for 1–2 hours, or until firm.

3 Dust your hands with a little cocoa powder and roll small pieces of the mixture into 1 inch (2.5cm) balls. If the mixture becomes too soft to roll, return it to the refrigerator to firm up.

4 Chill in the refrigerator until required.

ACTIVELY GOOD

NUTMEG HAS BEEN USED FOR ITS HEALING PROPERTIES SINCE ANCIENT TIMES. IT IS AN EFFECTIVE SEDATIVE, CALMING FRAYED NERVES, RELIEVING DEPRESSION, AND HELPING YOU TO SLEEP. NUTMEG CAN ALSO OFFER RELIEF FROM INFLAMED OR ACHING JOINTS AND MUSCLES.

HONEY

Nature's sweetener is more than just sweet—honey can heal and promote good health in an amazing array of ways. It can boost your immune system, balance your blood sugar levels and combat cholesterol, too.

To get the most from honey's beneficial properties, look for honey made in the summer from bees fed on flowers—farmers' markets and health food stores are the best places to shop for really good honey. Better still, choose raw honey, which has had only the bare minimum of processing since it was harvested from the hive. There is evidence to suggest that phytonutrients found in raw honey may help to prevent some cancers and inhibit the growth of tumors.

It is for less severe ailments that honey is best known as a natural cure. If you suffer from hayfever, eating locally produced honey—from bees that have fed on the flowers that are causing your allergy—may help to relieve your symptoms and prevent subsequent attacks. And a spoonful of honey is a time-honored solution to night-time coughing in children with common coughs and colds.

Honey is a much better choice as a sweetener than sucrose or glucose if you need to consider controlling blood sugar levels, as it does not cause such a spike and later dip in your sugars. For this reason, diabetics can often tolerate honey better than other sugars, so the candies in this section may be particularly well suited to them.

Honey also contains antioxidants, which can help to improve heart health and promote healthy blood vessels, and this can help to prevent strokes as well as heart disease.

- **Honeycomb toffee** is a simple and delicious homemade candy: there are two different recipes on pages 118 and 119. Try dipping your finished pieces in melted chocolate or break them into crumbs to use as a topping for cheesecake, ice cream, or more.
- Make the most of the natural sugars in honey by mixing honey with dried fruits, such as in the **Honeyed Fruit Bars** (page 116). They are perfect for a quick and healthy energy boost when you feel yourself flagging.
- Honey also makes a delicious brittle when boiled to hardball stage. Try **Honey and Hazelnut Caramel** (page 116), which has the added benefit of nuts, which can help to regulate the healthy cholesterol levels in your body and combat the bad LDL cholesterol.

Honey and Hazelnut Caramel

NUTS ADDS TEXTURE TO THIS BRITTLE CARAMEL, AND OLEIC ACID, WHICH CAN
LOWER 'BAD' LDL CHOLESTEROL AND PROMOTE 'GOOD' HDL CHOLESTEROL.

You will need

- ½ cup (170g) clear honey
- A generous ½ cup (120ml) light corn syrup
- 6 tablespoons (90g) unsalted butter, diced
- 1 cup (150g) chopped hazelnuts

Makes about 1lb (450g)

1 Oil a cake pan 6 inch (15cm) square and put a candy thermometer in a bowl of hot water to warm.

2 Gently heat the honey, syrup and butter in a heavy saucepan, stirring with a wooden spoon, until they have melted.

3 Bring to a boil, and boil for 3 minutes. Put the candy thermometer in the saucepan and continue to boil until the temperature of the mixture reaches 265°F (129°C), the hard ball stage.

4 Remove the saucepan from the heat and carefully dip the base in cold water to stop the cooking.

5 Stir the nuts into the mixture, then pour it into the prepared cake pan and leave until the mixture is just beginning to set.

6 Mark the caramel into squares with a lightly oiled, sharp knife and leave to set completely. Then break into pieces, wrap individually in wax paper, and store in an airtight container.

OPPOSITE: HONEY AND HAZELNUT CARAMEL

Honeyed Fruit Bars

THESE CHEWY BARS ARE PACKED WITH NATURAL SUGARS. DRIED APRICOTS ARE HIGH
IN VITAMIN A, WHICH WILL HELP TO MAINTAIN A HEALTHY IMMUNE SYSTEM.

You will need

- ⅔ cup (100g) plumped dried apricots
- ½ cup (75g) dried pears
- 2½ tablespoons (40g) low-fat soft cheese
- 4 tablespoons carob powder
- 1½ tablespoons clear honey

Makes 18

1 Lightly oil a baking sheet or line it with wax paper and finely chop the dried fruit. Beat the soft cheese in a bowl until it is smooth, then beat in the carob powder and honey.

2 Stir in just under half of the chopped fruit and press half of this mixture onto the baking sheet in a square. Cover this with the remaining dried fruit and then the remaining cheese mixture, pressing the layers together with your hand or a spatula.

3 Wrap the square in wax paper and refrigerate until it is firm, then cut into bars to serve.

Honeycomb

THIS HONEYCOMB RECIPE IS MADE IN A MICROWAVE, BUT YOU CAN COOK IT IN A SAUCEPAN IF YOU PREFER. CRUMBLE HONEYCOMB INTO HOMEMADE ICE CREAM OR SPRINKLE IT OVER AS A TOPPING, OR DIP PIECES IN MELTED CHOCOLATE FOR A TREAT.

You will need

- $^2/_3$ cup (150ml) water
- 1 cup (190g) sugar
- 1 tablespoon light corn syrup
- ¼ teaspoon cream of tartar
- ½ teaspoon baking soda

Makes about ½lb (225g)

1 Oil a cake pan approximately 7 inch (18cm) square and put a candy thermometer in a bowl of hot water to warm up for later.

2 Heat the water in a large, microwave-safe bowl on High power for 2 minutes. Stir in the sugar, syrup and cream of tartar, heat on High power for 1 minute, then stir until the sugar has dissolved.

3 Heat on High for a further 10 minutes, checking the temperature with the candy thermometer every few minutes until the mixture reaches 310°F (154°C), the hard crack stage (see page 21).

4 Just before the syrup is ready, blend the baking soda with 1 teaspoon hot water in a small bowl.

5 Carefully stir the baking soda liquid into the hot syrup. The mixture will fizz and expand. Quickly pour it into the prepared cake pan and leave until the honeycomb is just beginning to set.

6 If you want regular pieces, mark into squares with a lightly oiled knife before you leave the honeycomb to set completely.

7 Break into pieces and store in an airtight container.

Honeycomb Toffee

THIS TRADITIONAL CINDER TOFFEE RECIPE IS A CHEWIER VERSION OF THE LIGHT HONEYCOMB OPPOSITE. WORK QUICKLY AND LIGHTLY ONCE YOU HAVE ADDED THE BAKING SODA SO THAT THE MIXTURE STAYS LIGHT AND AIRY.

You will need

- 2 cups (380g) sugar
- 4 tablespoons vinegar
- 3 tablespoons light corn syrup
- 1¼ cups (280ml) water
- ½ teaspoon baking soda

Makes about 1lb (450g)

1 Butter or oil a cake pan approximately 8 inch (20cm) square and put a candy thermometer in a bowl of hot water to warm.

2 Gently heat the sugar, vinegar, and syrup with the water in a large, heavy saucepan, stirring with a wooden spoon until the sugar has dissolved and the syrup has melted.

3 Bring to a boil, and boil for 3 minutes.

4 Add the candy thermometer to the saucepan and continue to boil until the temperature reaches 285°F (141°C), the soft crack stage (see page 21).

5 Remove the pan from the heat and carefully stir in the baking soda, mixing well to allow the bubbles to subside a little. Be prepared for the mixture to fizz and bubble up considerably.

6 Pour the mixture into the prepared cake pan and leave until it is just beginning to set.

7 Mark into squares with a lightly oiled, sharp knife and leave to set completely.

8 Cut or break into pieces. Wrap individually in wax paper, twisting the ends together, and store in an airtight container.

COOK'S NOTES

Substitute golden syrup or dark maple syrup if you cannot get light corn syrup, or you can also use clear, runny honey. Take care when measuring the baking soda—if you add too much, the honeycomb toffee will have a bitter taste of soda.

FLOWERS

FLOWERS ARE NOT A COMMON INGREDIENT IN COOKING, BUT SOME FLOWERS ARE
EDIBLE AND THEY ADD A DELICATE FLAVOR AND A REALLY PRETTY TOUCH TO THESE
CANDIES. ALWAYS CHECK THAT IT IS SAFE BEFORE EATING ANYTHING YOU PICK.

Roses and violets are the most commonly used edible flowers, but nasturtiums, lavender, marigolds, and many more can also be crystallized like **Sugared Violets** (page 122) or used in cooking. Their main use is as decoration on candies and cakes; for making most of the candies on the following pages you will need ingredients derived from the flowers, such as rosewater, rosehip syrup, and violet extract. If you cannot find these in your local grocery store, try healthfood stores and specialist cake decorating suppliers. If you choose to buy online, take care to avoid oils intended for use as a fragrance—you must only use food-grade ingredients. If in doubt, always check before you buy.

- Rosehip syrup is a traditional remedy for colds and a winter preventative to keep them at bay. Weight-for-weight it has 20 times as much vitamin C as orange juice, so the rosehips can help to boost your immune system and protect you against allergies.
- If you can't find any rosehip syrup in the stores for your **Rose Creams** (page 124), make your own. For 2lb (900g) rosehips you will need the same weight of sugar. Chop the rosehips and add them to 4 pints (2 liters) boiling water in a large saucepan. Bring the

water back to the boil, then remove from the heat and leave the hips to steep for 30 minutes. Pour the mixture through a jelly-straining bag or cheesecloth-lined strainer, then put the pulp back into the saucepan with 2 pints (1 liter) water and repeat the process. Put both quantities of juice in a clean saucepan and bring to the boil, then continue to boil until the volume has reduced by half. Remove the pan from the heat and stir in the sugar until is has dissolved. Bring the sugared syrup to the boil and boil for 5 minutes, then bottle the finished syrup in sterilized bottles and seal. Use it in recipes, as a cordial, or poured over ice cream or pancakes.

- Rosewater can be found in the baking section of most good grocery stores. Use it to flavor some **Turkish Delight** (page 125). Rosewater is a good source of antioxidants, which can help to keep your skin healthy.

Violet Creams

MAKE A BATCH OF THESE PRETTY CANDIES TO ACCOMPANY SOME ROSE CREAMS
(SEE PAGE 124). TAKE CARE TO BUY FOOD GRADE VIOLET EXTRACT, NOT THE FRAGRANCE
OIL: CAKE DECORATING SUPPLIERS ARE A GOOD PLACE TO FIND IT.

You will need

○ A few drops of violet extract
○ A few drops of natural violet food coloring
○ 8oz (225g) fondant (any variety, see pages 24–25)
○ Crystallized violets, for decoration (see below)

Makes about ½lb (225g)

1 Knead the violet extract and food coloring into the fondant and leave to dry for 1 hour.

2 Shape the fondant into small balls and flatten each one lightly.

3 Place a crystallized violet in the center of each and leave to dry for 24 hours.

Sugared Violets

YOU CAN FOLLOW THIS PROCESS TO CRYSTALLIZE ANY EDIBLE FLOWER OR PETAL,
SUCH AS INDIVIDUAL ROSE PETALS FOR DECORATING ROSE CREAMS (PAGE 124). YOU
WILL NEED A SMALL, CLEAN, AND SOFT ARTIST'S PAINT BRUSH FOR THIS DELICATE JOB.

You will need

○ 20–30 fresh violets
○ 1 large egg white
○ 1 tablespoon water
○ 1 cup (225g) superfine sugar

Makes 20–30 sugared violets

1 Preheat the oven to its lowest setting and line a baking sheet with parchment paper.

2 In a bowl, whisk the egg white with the water until it is just frothy.

3 Place the sugar in a shallow dish.

4 Carefully hold a violet between your thumb and one finger, and—very gently—use a paint brush dipped in the egg white mixture to paint the flower until you have covered it completely.

5 Hold the violet over the sugar dish and gently sprinkle sugar evenly all over on both sides—don't dip it in, or you will squash it. Place the sugared violet on the prepared baking sheet and repeat with the remaining flowers.

6 Place in the oven overnight, with the door ajar. Remove from the oven and cool, then store the finished sugared violets in an airtight container.

OPPOSITE: SUGARED VIOLETS

Rose Creams

THESE DELICATELY FLAVORED CREAMS HAVE AN OLD-TIME APPEAL. ROSEHIPS
CONTAIN BIOFLAVONOIDS WHICH CAN BOOST THE IMMUNE SYSTEM AND HELP
TO FIGHT OFF VIRUSES AND ALLERGIES, AND THEY ARE HIGH IN VITAMIN C.

You will need

○ 5 teaspoons lemon juice
○ ½ teaspoon finely grated lemon zest
○ 4 teaspoons rosehip syrup
○ A few drops of rosewater
○ Scant 2 cups (260g) confectioners' sugar,
sifted, plus extra for dusting
○ Crystallized rose petals, for decoration
(see instructions for Sugared Violets, page 122)

Makes about ½lb (225g)

1 Mix the lemon juice, zest, rosehip syrup, and rosewater together. Add the confectioners' sugar and work to a stiff mixture using your fingertips.

2 Break off small pieces of the mixture and roll into balls, dusting with extra, sifted confectioners' sugar.

3 Flatten each ball slightly and place a crystallized rose petal on top. Press lightly in place.

4 Place the creams in small paper candy cases and leave in a cool place to dry. If you prefer, dip the creams in melted chocolate (see page 32).

Turkish Delight

THIS JELLY WITH THE DELICATE FLAVOR OF ROSE IS A MIDDLE EASTERN TREAT
THAT IS EASY TO RECREATE AT HOME. IT TAKES A LITTLE TIME TO DO IT RIGHT,
BUT IT'S WORTH THE EFFORT AND MAKES A BEAUTIFUL GIFT IN A PRETTY BOX.

You will need

- Sunflower oil, for greasing
- 1 tablespoon lemon juice
- 4 cups (800g) sugar
- 3½ cups (875ml) water
- 1 cup (120g) cornstarch
- 1 teaspoon cream of tartar
- 1 tablespoon rosewater
- Mixture of 1 part cornstarch to 5 parts confectioners' sugar, for dusting

Makes about 80 pieces

1 Put a candy thermometer in hot water to warm, and lightly oil an 8 inch (20cm) cake pan. Line the pan with parchment paper and lightly oil the paper.

2 Place the lemon juice, sugar, and 1½ cups (375ml) water in a heavy saucepan and bring to the boil, stirring to dissolve the sugar. Add the candy thermometer and keep boiling until the mixture reaches 234°F (112°C), the softball stage (page 21).

3 Remove the syrup from the heat and, in a second saucepan, mix together 2 cups (500ml) water, the cornstarch and cream of tartar. Use a whisk to remove any lumps. Bring the cornstarch mixture to the boil, stirring, until it is a sticky paste, then—little by little—add the hot syrup, still whisking. Bring to the boil again, then simmer for 1 hour, stirring often.

4 Add the rosewater to the finished syrup, then pour it into the prepared cake pan and leave it to cool overnight. Turn out the set jelly and dust it liberally all over with the combined cornstarch and confectioners' sugar, then cut into squares with an oiled, sharp knife. Store the candy in an airtight container with any remaining cornstarch and confectioners' sugar dusting mixture.

INDEX

Quantum would like to thank and acknowledge the following for supplying the pictures reproduced in this book:

iStock page 107

Shutterstock pages 4, 5, 55, 77, 87, 99, 115, 121

Stockfood pages 2, 5, 7, 9, 14, 30, 41, 42, 43, 45, 46, 48, 51, 52, 57, 60, 62, 64, 65, 67, 68, 73, 74, 79, 80, 83, 85, 89, 90, 91, 93, 95, 101, 103, 105, 108, 111, 112, 113, 117, 118, 123, 125

All other photographs and illustrations are the copyright of Quantum Publishing Ltd.

While every effort has been made to credit contributors, Quantum would like to apologize should there have been any omissions or errors.